SIMONE DE BEAUVOIR

A BEGINNER'S GUIDE

ALISON HOLLAND

Series Editors
Rob Abbott & Charlie Bell

Hodder & Stoughton

A MEMBER OF THE HODDER HEADLINE GROUP

Orders: please contact Bookpoint Ltd, 130 Milton Park, Abingdon, Oxon OX14 4SB. Telephone: +44 (0) 1235 827720, Fax: +44 (0) 1235 400454. Lines are open from 9.00–6.00, Monday to Saturday, with a 24-hour message answering service. Email address: orders@bookpoint.co.uk

British Library Cataloguing in Publication Data
A catalogue record for this title is available from The British Library

ISBN 0 340 85040 X

First published 2002
Impression number   10 9 8 7 6 5 4 3 2 1
Year 2007 2006 2005 2004 2003 2002

Cover photo from Hulton/Archive, photographer Studio Harcourt.
Typeset by Transet Limited, Coventry, England.
Printed in Great Britain for Hodder & Stoughton Educational, a division of Hodder Headline Plc, 338 Euston Road, London NW1 3BH by Cox & Wyman, Reading, Berks.

CONTENTS

Beauvoir's Life

EARLY YEARS

Simone Lucie Ernestine Marie Bertrand de Beauvoir was born in Paris
on 9 January 1908. Her parents, Françoise and Georges de Beauvoir,
were members of the well-to-do bourgeoisie (upper middle class),
albeit from the less well-to-do, less well-regarded side of the family.
George, a lawyer, disdained hard work and was a dandy at heart; his
passion was for the theatre. The codes they lived by were nevertheless
rigid and appearances were all important. Although Georges was an
open atheist, Françoise was a devout Catholic and it was she who
dominated her daughters' upbringing.

Simone de Beauvoir's first home above the café La Rotonde on the Boulevard du
Montparnasse.

Simone was a precocious child who loved being the centre of attention.
As a young child, she was pretty with long, thick, curly hair and big,
blue eyes. If she did not get her own way, she would have noisy temper
tantrums, holding her breath until her face turned red or even making
herself vomit. When Simone was two-and-a-half, her sister, Hélène,
was born on 9 June 1910. A petite, pretty, doll-like child, she was given
the pet name, Poupette, which means 'little doll' in French. The sisters
were very close.

Simone was an unpopular child at school. The most significant friendship during her childhood was with her intellectual equal, Elisabeth Lacoin (Zaza Mabille in the memoirs). Their friendship lasted into their twenties, despite the opposition of Zaza's mother, who considered Simone to be a bad influence on her daughter. She was determined that Zaza would marry well. When Zaza died suddenly and mysteriously at the age of 21 as she was about to be sent to Berlin, away from an unsuitable match, Simone would feel that she had paid for her own freedom with Zaza's death.

EDUCATION

Simone attended a private Catholic school for girls, *le cours Désir*. The teaching was mediocre and emphasis was laid on preparing the girls either for marriage and motherhood or for the veil. Simone adored learning and read whatever she could. Simone's father enjoyed the fact that he had a clever daughter 'with a man's brain' and would introduce her to less pious books and engage her in discussion.

It was a change for the worse in family fortunes after World War I that both ended the domestic harmony in which the family had lived until then and, simultaneously, opened up Simone's future. After the war, Georges de Beauvoir could no longer afford to practise law and had to rely on poorly paid jobs, working for the financial pages of several newspapers. In 1919, when Simone was eleven-and-a-half, financial difficulties meant the family had to leave their first-floor apartment on the Boulevard Montparnasse and move to a much smaller, cheaper, fifth-floor appartment in the Rue de Rennes. It was around this time that Simone's father announced to his daughters that they would not be able to marry as they would have no dowries and that they would need to study because they would have to earn their livings.

TEENAGE YEARS

Aged 14, Simone lost her faith in God. Her initial calm gave way to panic and despair as she realized that the logical implication was that she was condemned to die. Alone in the house, she threw herself on the floor and tore at the carpet, screaming. She would experience such emotional crises and remain morbidly obsessed by death for the rest of her life.

Simone's father was disappointed to see his daughter becoming an intellectual; while he valued creativity and learning for its own sake, he despised teachers as lower-middle-class upstarts and imputed politically dangerous ideas to intellectuals. He transferred his affection to Poupette who was much prettier and more feminine than her elder sister and as well as more 'artistic', a quality he prized. His rejection badly hurt Simone and she remembered all her life, her father's cruel comment to her when she was twelve, that she was ugly. She experienced her mother as jealous and intrusive.

Simone's older cousin, Jacques Champigneulles, was an important person during her teen years. He was an independent-minded young man who talked to the Beauvoir sisters about books and ideas. For a time, Simone thought she loved him and, despite her lack of dowry, there was an expectation that she would marry him one day.

STUDIES

Simone decided on a career teaching philosophy. Her parents did not approve of her decision, but Simone's stubborn refusal to consider any other career forced them to relent. Simone's mother allowed her to enrol at the Sorbonne University in Paris, but arranged for her to prepare for her degree mostly at Catholic institutes. After completing her undergraduate studies in 1928, Beauvoir went on to write a thesis on Leibniz and to prepare the **agrégation**, the very competitive postgraduate examination for teaching posts in *lycées* and universities. Beauvoir gravitated towards the most gifted students in her year, including Maurice Merleau-Ponty and Jean-Paul Sartre. In particular, she became very close to René Maheu, who was married. Close friends

KEYWORDS

Agrégation: Competitive postgraduate examination for teaching posts in *lycées* and universities.

Lycée: State secondary school.

believed he was Beauvoir's first lover, but she always insisted that their friendship remained intellectual. Maheu first gave her the nickname Castor, a translation into French of the English word 'beaver', because of the way she worked so hard. When Simone graduated in 1929, she was only the ninth woman in France ever to become an *agrégée* of philosophy.

JEAN-PAUL SARTRE

According to her memoirs, Beauvoir found in Sartre a dream-companion, her double, someone with whom she could share everything. The myth she constructed of her fundamental unity with Sartre was crucial to Beauvoir's sense of identity and protected her from a sense of loss, loneliness and despair. Writing in her sixties, she would refer to her meeting with Sartre as the most important event in her life. She considered him to be intellectually superior, discounting her own achievements in order to be able to do so. Beauvoir and Sartre agreed pacts of freedom and openness:

* Their love would be *necessary* but they would also have **contingent** loves, that is incidental relationships with others.

* They would tell each other everything.

> **KEYWORD**
>
> Contingent: Something which occurs which might not have occurred.

In reality, their relationship was lopsided. Beauvoir systematically put Sartre's needs before her own. At times, she suffered dreadful pangs of jealousy when she feared that she might lose the special place she had in Sartre's life to another woman. Sartre had no qualms about lying to Beauvoir. For her part, she never confronted him with his lies but 'let him off the hook', retreating behind a wall of politeness. As well as being his intellectual confidant, critic and editor, Beauvoir saw it as her role to protect Sartre. He was incapable of saying 'no', especially to women, and she was prepared to play the 'baddy' by saying 'no' for him.

Perceptions of their relationship have changed over the years. Certainly, they offered an unconventional model of a relationship.

Beauvoir refused marriage, monogamy, motherhood and even a shared domestic life, both of them living for many years in separate rooms on different floors in a series of rather cheap hotels. Later, feminists questioned Beauvoir's loyalty to Sartre and asked what made her stay with a misogynist.

He undoubtedly provided the intellectual support she needed but the drawback has been that Beauvoir has tended to be seen as his disciple. It is undeniably the case that Beauvoir published no work of her own until 1943 when she was 35 years old and until that time was known as 'only Sartre's girlfriend' – sometimes unflatteringly referred to as *La Grande Sartreuse* or *Notre Dame de Sartre* by hostile critics. The passionate, not to say acrimonious debate about the extent to which the couple borrowed from each other's work is ongoing. Beauvoir herself downplays her own originality and is content to be seen as an advocate of Sartre's philosophy. While it may be true that Beauvoir uses Sartre's work as a reference point in her work, her emphases are different and she sometimes disagrees with him. We know that Beauvoir worked very closely indeed with Sartre on his manuscripts, but the question of her actual contribution to his work remains; Beauvoir herself was reluctant to discuss this, but in the case of Sartre's journalism, there is evidence that her role did occasionally extend beyond that of editing to actually writing in his place.

The publication of Sartre's letters to Beauvoir in 1983 and, after her death, of Beauvoir's letters to Sartre and her war diary in 1990, led to a reassessment of their relationship. The letters revealed a gap between the myth of the professional, writing couple and reality. Many were shocked at their apparent disregard for the feelings of others, as the couple frankly confided in each other about their contingent loves.

EARLY CAREER

In 1929, Beauvoir escaped from the family home to live in a room she rented from her grandmother, supporting herself by working as a part-time teacher. This freedom was bliss. She spent the years 1931–43 teaching philosophy in *lycées*, first in Marseilles (until 1932), then in Rouen and finally, from 1936, in Paris. (The French system of filling teaching posts meant that separation from Sartre was inevitable unless they married.) Beauvoir was an unconventional teacher and her relationship with the authorities and her colleagues were strained. The pre-war years in Paris were dominated by teaching, largely unsuccessful attempts at writing and intense relationships within a circle of close friends. Then and always, cafés were a focal point in her existence; there she would eat, work, write letters, meet friends and rub shoulders with well-known writers, artists, actors and actresses, and intellectuals.

THE FAMILY

Throughout their lives, Beauvoir and Sartre surrounded themselves with younger men and women whose existences they would annexe to their own. The young men were Sartre's disciples, and many of the young women became his lovers. The couple and their entourage referred to themselves as the Family. Included in the circle were some of Beauvoir's former pupils. Beauvoir's teaching career ended in 1943 when the mother of one of her pupils, Nathalie Sorokine, (Natasha, as Beauvoir called her), complained to the authorities about Beauvoir's immoral influence over their daughter. After the war she was offered reinstatement but declined in order to devote herself to writing.

OLGA KOSAKIEVICZ

When she was in Rouen, an intense friendship developed between Beauvoir and one of her pupils, Olga Kosakievicz. When Sartre fell madly in love with Olga, they agreed to extend their couple into the 'trio'. The resulting complications and emotional distress dominated all their lives for years. Beauvoir's first novel, *She came to Stay*, would tell the story of the triangular relationship.

The situation became more complicated when, in July 1938, during a camping trip in the Alps, Beauvoir also began an intimate relationship with Jacques-Laurent Bost, a former student of Sartre's who was Olga's lover and later, her husband. Bost and Beauvoir would continue to be occasional lovers until the late 1940s. Although Beauvoir broke off their intimate relationship then, Bost would remain a close friend and ally until her death.

DARK TIMES

The emotional crises or bouts of crying linked to her loss of faith and fear of death, to which Beauvoir was prone, typically manifested themselves in public places. She would drink too much, then start to cry. Silent tears would give way to audible sobs that wracked her whole body. Then abruptly, Beauvoir would stop crying and join in the conversation again as if nothing had happened.

Beauvoir's fear of separation and loss led to repeated periods of depression and anxiety attacks. In her memoirs, Beauvoir describes how, periodically, she was ravaged by crises of despair where she would wallow in an abyss compounded of death, nothingness and infinity.

SEXUALITY

After the 'trio', Beauvoir had a number of contingent relationships with women, some of whom she shared with Sartre, notably her ex-students Nathalie Sorokine and Bianca Lamblin (*née* Bienenfield). She did not define herself as a lesbian as she did not desire women exclusively. Some of her readers have been disappointed by her lack of openness about her sexuality, as well as, it must be said, by the disparaging way in which she sometimes describes her liaisons with women to Sartre. In her letters she complains to him about the demands her 'charming vermin' make on her and claims not to enjoy having sexual relations with them. Be that as it may, she did not break off the relationships and the intensity of her feelings is clear. Towards the end of her life, Beauvoir regretted not having spoken about her sexuality more; she had come to see that it was a political as well as a personal issue.

WORLD WAR II

Sartre was called up in the summer of 1939 and Beauvoir would remain in Paris, carrying out her teaching duties. Much of her energy was devoted to meeting Sartre's needs; ensuring he had the paper, pens, ink, books and pipe tobacco he needed at the front. She put aside her own work to spend time reading the philosophers that would make her expert enough to help Sartre with his. The Family also made demands on her and looked to Beauvoir for direction in Sartre's absence. As for her own writing, Beauvoir had begun what would become *She Came to Stay*, her first published novel, in October 1938.

The **phoney war** ended abruptly with the German invasion of Western Europe in May 1940. After briefly joining the Exodus south to escape the German invaders, Beauvoir was back adjusting to life in a defeated, occupied Paris at the end of June. She spent her days teaching, reading in the *Bibliothèque Nationale* (French National Library), and writing in the Café de Flore or the Dôme.

KEYWORDS

Phoney war: The period between the declaration of World War II and the German invasion of Western Europe (September 1939 – March 1940).

Café du Dôme, Paris.

In March 1941, Sartre was released from the prison-camp where he had been held since the French defeat in June 1940. He came back changed by his experiences and keen to become involved in the Resistance. His attitude dismayed Beauvoir; she simply wanted to survive the war and found his ideas impractical not to say downright dangerous. The

The reading room at the French National Library.

resistance group they founded, *Socialisme et Liberté* (Socialism and Freedom), was ineffectual and short-lived, and better organized groups did not trust Sartre who was too visible and too indiscreet.

Both during and then after the war, damaging allegations were made against Sartre and thus against Beauvoir by association. Both were criticized for their lack of Resistance credentials and for continuing to publish and have their plays performed during the war. Moreover, once she had lost her teaching job, Beauvoir earned her living by working for Radio France, then controlled by the Nazis. Significantly, no formal accusations were made against them in the purge that followed the end of the war.

Around the time of Sartre's release, Georges de Beauvoir died. Beauvoir was saddened but not greatly affected by her father's death. The same year, 1941, *She Came to Stay* was accepted for publication by Gallimard. In writing *She Came to Stay*, Beauvoir found her voice and it seemed to her that in future, she would always have something to say. She wrote prolifically during the final years of the war. She immediately began work on her second novel, *The Blood of Others*, which was completed in 1943 and published in 1945. In 1943 she also wrote *Pyrrhus et Cinéas*, a philosophical essay, and began work on her third novel, *All Men are Mortal*. The year 1944 saw her one and only play, *Who Shall Die?*, written and performed.

LIBERATION AND THE POST-WAR DECADES

Paris was liberated on 25 August 1944. The success of *She Came to Stay* meant that Beauvoir was now a major intellectual figure in her own right. She and Sartre founded the weekly review, *Les Temps modernes* (Modern Times), in 1944. It became an influential forum for the expression of left-wing intellectual views. Much of the editorial work fell to Beauvoir and she was prevented from devoting much time to her own work.

From 1945, existentialism was fashionable and the label existentialist was applied to Beauvoir and Sartre. Sartre became involved in politics from 1946 and Beauvoir supported him.

Beauvoir, dubbed 'France's No. 2 Existentialist' in the American press, spent the first five months of 1947 on a lecture tour in the United States. She found much to like and admire in America and much to detest. Her lectures were well received, particularly in the women's colleges. Her impressions of her trip are recounted in *America Day by Day*, published in 1948.

NELSON ALGREN

During her trip to America, Beauvoir met Nelson Algren, a writer in Chicago. They became lovers. Beauvoir described her relationship with Algren as the one truly passionate relationship in her life; it was different from her relationship with Sartre but equally important. It was also the only relationship in which she played the traditional woman's role. She called herself 'his loving wife' and Algren her 'loving husband'. Beauvoir and Algren began corresponding in 1947 and would continue to correspond until 1964. Theirs would be a tempestuous, long-distance relationship with long periods of separation; Algren could not contemplate leaving Chicago and Beauvoir's life was in Paris with Sartre. It became increasingly difficult for Algren to accept the pact between Beauvoir and Sartre.

In 1951, during one of Beauvoir's visits, Algren told her he wished to end their relationship. Passionate love evolved into tender friendship and Algren came to play the same role for Beauvoir as she played for Sartre: attentive critic and intellectual ally. Their friendship came to a bitter end over the English translation of the third volume of her memoirs, *Force of Circumstance*. Algren, a very private man, had been angry over the American publication of *The Mandarins*, which in part, told the story of their love affair. He was absolutely furious over what Beauvoir wrote about him in her memoirs, so furious he broke off their correspondence. He would remain as angry as ever until he died suddenly of a massive heart attack in 1981. Beauvoir continued to wear his ring until she died and was buried with it still on her finger.

On her return from the United States, as well as *America Day by Day*, Beauvoir published *The Ethics of Ambiguity* (1947) and also a collection of philosophical essays, *L'Existentialisme et la sagesse des nations* (1948) (existentialism and the wisdom of nations). The main focus of her attention now was her 'book about women', which would become *The Second Sex*. With the publication of *The Second Sex* came notoriety. Beauvoir worked on her next project, the novel *The Mandarins*, from 1949 to 1953.

CLAUDE LANZMANN

In 1952, when she was feeling old and thought that all passion was behind her, Beauvoir began a relationship with Claude Lanzmann, a member of the *Les Temps modernes* team and 17 years her junior. Their intimate relationship would last until 1959 and they would remain close until Beauvoir's death. Lanzmann was the only man with whom Beauvoir ever cohabited, but during the seven years they spent as a couple, they both scrupulously avoided performing any domestic chores for each other. Lanzmann was a very positive influence in Beauvoir's life; she no longer felt old and her anxiety attacks were held at bay.

When *The Mandarins* was published in1954, Beauvoir was awarded France's most prestigious literary prize, the *Goncourt.* With some of the prize money, Beauvoir bought a large, one-roomed flat, overlooking Montparnasse cemetery.

It was two years after *The Mandarins* that Beauvoir's other commitments allowed her to think of writing again. In 1956, aged 48, she began writing her autobiography. The first volume, *Memoirs of a Dutiful Daughter* was published in 1958, the second, *The Prime of Life,* in 1960 and the third, *Force of Circumstance,* in 1963.

SYLVIE LE BON

In 1960, the year after Beauvoir separated from Lanzmann, Beauvoir met Sylvie Le Bon. Sylvie Le Bon was then 17, Beauvoir 52. Their intermittent and casual friendship developed into what Beauvoir called the strongest and most important friendship of her life, equal in importance to the one she shared with Sartre. For Sylvie Le Bon, it was love between them. Whether or not the relationship was sexual, they clearly made a life-long committment to each other. Sylvie Le Bon would remain Beauvoir's companion until she died.

Françoise de Beauvoir died of cancer in 1963. Beauvoir was deeply upset by her mother's death. Her reflex to deal with her pain and grief by writing about it, prompted her to write an account of her mother's life and death in *A Very Easy Death.*

Beauvoir turned to fiction again in 1965. From 1965 until 1967 she worked on *Les Belles Images* (1966) and *The Woman Destroyed* (1968) collection of short stories. Extracts of the title story 'The Woman Destroyed' appeared in *Elle* magazine with illustrations by her sister, Hélène, in 1967.

OLD AGE

The late 1960s and early 1970s were a very busy time for Beauvoir. The political isolation in which she and Sartre had found themselves since the end of the Algerian war, came to an end with the events of May 1968. During the student uprising, they supported the most militant of the students who were protesting against rigid hierarchies and the power the technocrats held in France at that time. The same radical political activism led Beauvoir to support banned revolutionary newspapers in the early 1970s. At around this time too, she began to support the anti-abortion campaigns of the newly formed French women's movement, *Mouvement de Libération des Femmes – MLF*. More than twenty years after the publication of *The Second Sex*, Beauvoir publicly declared herself to be a feminist.

During this period, Beauvoir channelled her creative energies into a study about the lives of the old, *Old Age* (1970), in many ways a parallel text to *The Second Sex*, and the final volume of her memoirs, *All Said and Done* (1972). The film, *Simone de Beauvoir*, was made in 1978. In 1979, Beauvoir decided to publish *When Things of the Spirit Come First*, a collection of short fiction completed in 1937.

SARTRE – FINAL YEARS

In the 1970s, the growing importance of Sylvie Le Bon in Beauvoir's life and her increasing commitment to feminist causes coincided with what would become an important shift in her relationship with Sartre. The public image of the successful writing couple was dear to Beauvoir and she was not prepared to admit that there had been any fundamental change. However, day to day, their worlds were becoming more distinct; Beauvoir's relations were increasingly difficult with Arlette Elkaïm, Sartre's companion and, subsequently, adoptive daughter, and with Benny Lévy (alias Pierre Victor), Sartre's secretary. It is also true that, as Sartre's health deteriorated, Beauvoir was relieved to be able to leave his care to others and to spend more time with Sylvie Le Bon. Later, Beauvoir said she regretted her 'selfishness'.

Sartre died in 1980. Beauvoir was grief stricken. Shortly after the funeral, she became ill with pneumonia and spent the next month in hospital. The situation was even more painful because of disagreements over Sartre's estate with Arlette Elkaïm-Sartre. Beauvoir remained seriously depressed for the next year. Typically, Beauvoir wrote to understand and come to terms with her pain. *Adieux:*

A Farewell to Sartre, an account of the last ten years of Sartre's life and protracted final illness, was published in 1981.

In 1980, in spite of the gossip she knew it would cause, Beauvoir adopted Sylvie Le Bon, who would thus become Beauvoir's literary executor. Her new surname was Le Bon de Beauvoir but she did not use it until after Beauvoir's death.

Beauvoir devoted the next few years to publishing Sartre's letters (*Lettres au Castor*) (this, despite the objections of Arlette), to working with feminists and to travelling with Sylvie Le Bon. By the end of 1985, Beauvoir's health was deteriorating; she found it extremely difficult to walk and the cirrhosis of her liver, caused by her excess consumption of whisky, was worsening. However, she remained mentally well until the end of her life.

Beauvoir survived Sartre by almost six years to the day. She died in hospital after a short illness on 14 April 1986, aged 78. She was buried in Montparnasse cemetery next to Sartre on 19 April. The funeral was attended by Beauvoir's family and close friends, together with some five thousand people, many of them women who had come from all over the world.

❋ ❋ ❋ SUMMARY ❋ ❋ ❋

- Beauvoir lived from January 1908 to April 1986. Most of her life was spent in Paris.

- She was born into a conservative, upper-middle-class family, but became a radical, left-wing intellectual.

- She was a brilliant student. After graduating, she taught philosophy until 1943.

- She wanted to become a writer, initially dedicating herself to literature. Her writing included philosophy, fiction, and auto-biography.

- She met Sartre in 1929 and he became her life-long companion. Their relationship was not monogamous and she had other relationships, notably with Algren, Lanzmann and Sylvie Le Bon.

- Beauvoir supported radical causes. In the 1970s, she publicly defined herself as a feminist and supported the newly formed French women's movement, MLF.

Philosophy 2

Beauvoir loved philosophy. For her, philosophy was the best of all possible subjects. In her memoirs, Beauvoir writes:

> The thing that attracted me about philosophy was that it went straight to essentials. [...] I had always wanted to know *everything*; philosophy would allow me to appease this desire, for it aimed at total reality; philosophy went right to the heart of truth and revealed to me [...] an order, a reason, a necessity in everything. The sciences, literature and all the other disciplines seeemed to me to be very poor relations to philosophy.
>
> (*Memoirs of a Dutiful Daughter*, p. 158)

However, loving philosophy was not enough to become a philosopher, she said. According to her memoirs, in 1929, Simone de Beauvoir, the brilliant philosophy student, decided that she would dedicate herself to literature, ostensibly leaving philosophy to Sartre, whom she considered to be a more original thinker than herself. This 'decision' is contradicted by the passionate commitment to doing philosophy that emerges from Beauvoir's student diaries of the time. In reality, she did not so much give up philosophy for literature, as pursue her project of doing philosophy through literature.

There is widespread agreement that Beauvoir is a major thinker of the twentieth century because of the contribution *The Second Sex* has made to the theorizing of the social and political revolution in women's roles but, until recently, little critical attention had been paid to her philosophy and she has been undervalued and ignored as a philosopher. There are a number of possible explanations for this:

* Beauvoir's own representation of her intellectual status: she did not define herself as a philosopher in her memoirs and later interviews.

* Sexism means that she is seen simply as Sartre's disciple and her originality is ignored because of her relationship with him.

* The marginalized situation of women in relation to the discipline of philosophy and the tendency to exclude them from the philosophical **canon**. Still today, despite her major contribution to **existentialism**, Beauvoir is generally ignored or else mentioned only in relation to Sartre in histories of philosophy or studies of existentialism.

> **KEYWORDS**
>
> Canon: Writings that are considered to be of lasting significance.
>
> Existentialism: Philosophy according to which existence precedes essence and which insists on human freedom and responsibility.

However, it is important to bear in mind the following points:

* When Beauvoir said she was not a philosopher, she was defining the term in a very narrow way to mean someone who creates a philosophical system. Her comments in interviews and her memoirs make it clear that she did consider herself to be a philosopher in the sense that she had studied and taught philosophy, was infused with philosophy and that philosophy was her way of seeing the world.

* It can be argued that some of the key ideas of French **existentialism** were originally Beauvoir's, not Sartre's. Scholarly research has now begun to challenge traditional assumptions and to study Beauvoir's philosophy as distinct from Sartre's. Only when her own philosophical development has been traced, will it be possible to present a full picture of the Beauvoir/Sartre philosophical relationship and adjudicate fairly the argument about their relative contributions.

PHILOSOPHICAL PRACTICE

Beauvoir developed her philosophical thought, not only in her formal philosophical writings, but in all of her other writings too. Since she attached a great deal of importance to her work as a novelist, she engaged with philosophical questions and developed her philosophical ideas in her fiction, particularly. For her, there was no boundary between literature and philosophy. She saw them both as expressions of a writer's view of the world. As a philosophy student in 1927, Beauvoir was already imagining a philosophical methodology which would allow her to write essays on life that would combine fiction and philosophy, and where the search for truth would be paramount. Importantly, Beauvoir used her own experience as a basis for her philosophical ideas. This is related to her rejection of universalism – no one can take a universal or God-like point of view, she argues, as each of us can only speak from our own individual human experience. At the same time, Beauvoir rejects the authoritarianism of traditional philosophy, insisting on readers' freedom of thought.

Beauvoir's methodology, outlined in 'Littérature et métaphysique' (Literature and metaphysics), is rooted in the existentialist tradition in which abstract ideas and general principles are arrived at through particular concrete examples. As an existentialist philosopher, Beauvoir's role is to describe the world so that its meanings emerge. Since the world as a whole cannot be described, she must focus on detailed examples which will reveal significances.

KEY QUESTIONS

Beauvoir's philosophical inquiry focuses chiefly on **metaphysics** and **ethics**. She is interested in problems to do with human consciousness and its relation with:

* the body

* its own past, present and future

* the world

* other consciousnesses.

KEYWORDS

Metaphysics: Philosophy to do with our relations with the world and other consciousnesses.

Ethics: Philosophical inquiry into or theory of standards of right and wrong, good and bad in respect of character and conduct.

The questions Beauvoir asks are questions typical of modern philosophy:

* What is the relation between an individual's freedom and their situation?

* What is the nature of self-identity?

* How is the individual related to society?

* What is the individual's relation to the world?

* How can moral chioces be made in the absence of universal moral absolutes, such as divine commandments?

KEY PRINCIPLES

From reading Beauvoir's writings as a whole, we can glean her central philosophical ideas.

Metaphysics

* **Consciousness** is not a kind of being in the world, but a relation with or to the world – consciousness is always consciousness of something. This is referred to as **intentionality**.

* Consciounesses exist in bodies (embodiment) and are separated from each other.

* In terms of **ontology**, from the point of view of an individual consciousness, there are two primary categories of being: non-conscious being which includes anything at all that can be an object of consciousness; conscious being which is synonymous with human being.

* There are two dimensions to human reality: **immanence** (the givens of our situation)

KEYWORDS

Consciousness: (Mind), the relation we have with the world.

Intentionality: The relation between consciousness and real and imagined objects in the world.

Ontology: The branch of philosophy concerned with being.

Immanence: When we think of ourselves as things in the world and are confined by the givens of our situation.

and **transcendance** (freedom).

KEYWORDS

Transcendence: Existence characterized by freedom and directed to what is beyond ourselves.

Intersubjectivity: The philosophical problem of the existence of other minds.

* There is no such thing as our true self somewhere inside us. The self is a narrative construct – a story we tell ourselves – which is always evolving, always in the process of becoming (emergent). (This is not to say that we cannot have a deeper, truer sense of ourselves when we probe beneath the veneer of our social identities.)

* **Intersubjectivity**: individuals exist and relate to each other as subjects (perceiving consciousnesses) and objects (what is perceived). This subject/object split characterizes human existence.

* All of us may be objectified, that is become the object term of the subject/object relation.

* Both terms of the intersubjective relation may be social groups – men/women, whites/blacks. Members of an oppressed social group experience themselves as the negatively defined object term of the subject/object relation.

Ethics

* The human condition is ambiguous in the sense that we exist simultaneously in the objective and subjective, body and consciousness, in society and as an individual, and in eternity and as mortal.

* We must reject all moral absolutes and instead of taking our moral standards from God, invent them for ourselves.

* Values do not exist independently of consciousness.

* As individuals, we bring value into the world through the objects and goals we freely choose.

* Human freedom is the source of all value and meaning.

* Freedom is situational in the sense that we are free to choose our projects in a world of givens – some situations afford us more freedom to realize our goals than others.

* Freedom is not a given state but one we must struggle to maintain – a permanent process of liberation.

* Consciousnesses are interdependent because we define ourselves in relation to others and also because we exist in societies that define and evaluate individuals and groups in relation to each other, in terms of specific criteria.

* In terms of the subject/object relation, **subjection** is the struggle between individuals or groups for subjective domination, the power to define others. **Reciprocity** is where, as individuals or groups, we recognize each other's freedom and treat each other both as subject and object.

* It is in our self-interest to respect and promote the freedom of others who we need to validate and carry forward our projects. Besides, others give meaning to the world, so making it a place where our self-realization is possible.

KEYWORDS

Subjection: The struggle between individuals or groups for subjective domination.

Reciprocity: When individuals or groups recognize each other's freedom and treat each other both as subject and object.

Beauvoir thinks that to act morally, we must:

* fight oppression in whatever way our situation allows

* be prepared to use violence to preserve freedom

* set ourselves concrete, finite goals that are justified in themselves, not in terms of an indefinite future

* act in such a way as to prevent more harm than we inflict

* accept responsibility for our actions.

Beauvoir defined herself as an existentialist and her key philosophical ideas permeate and are permeated by the philosophy identified with Sartre.

EXISTENTIALISM

Existentialism is the philosophy expounded by Sartre in his *Being and Nothingness* (1943). It was during the same time that Sartre was working on his philosophical ideas that Beauvoir was working on her novel, *She Came to Stay*. We know that she gave up her own work for a time to read philosophers whose work would help her to help Sartre with his and collaborated with him on every single page of the manuscript of *Being and Nothingness*. It is hardly surprising then, that *She Came to Stay* and *Being and Nothingness* have a number of themes in common and share the same philosophical framework, reflecting Beauvoir's and Sartre's shared background in French philosophy, from Descartes to Bergson, and German philosophy, including Kant, Hegel, Husserl and Heidegger. Scholars are still researching the question of philosophical influence – who influenced whom?

Timings

Considerable attention has been paid to the question of when *She Came to Stay* and *Being and Nothingness* were actually written, as this impinges on our appreciation of Beauvoir's input to existentialism and her intellectual subservience or otherwise. Sartre's essay was published several months before Beauvoir's novel, in the summer of 1943. However, when Beauvoir submitted her manuscript to the publishers in October 1941, Sartre had only just begun writing *Being and Nothingness*. In fact, evidence from Sartre's war diaries and his correspondence with Beauvoir, suggests that the breakthrough in the development of his philosophical system came in February 1940, following his army leave, during which he read the manuscript of *She Came to Stay*.

Existentialism has engendered a complex terminology but this need not be a barrier to understanding the basic concepts. The starting point for existentialism is Heidegger's idea that existence precedes **essence**. This means that we, as human beings, define what it means to be human by our actions. To exist is to project ourselves into the future. The result of this is that the self can never be identical with itself – as Bergson said, it is always in the process of becoming. Freedom is inescapable. We are free to make choices about our being but not making a choice is impossible; by not choosing we are still making choices about who we will be. The things we choose to do in the world are our **projects** and when, through them, we are oriented towards things beyond ourselves, this is transcendence. We act with **authenticity** if we acknowledge our freedom and take responsibility for our actions, thus thinking of ourselves as a transcendent consciousness (also referred to as **for-itself**) as opposed to thinking of ourselves as mere things in the world (referred to as immanence, **in-itself** or **facticity**). Alongside freedom (transcendance), immanence is the second dimension of human existence. Immanence is best understood as the givens of our existence, such as our bodies with their fixed sex, race and heredity, our place in a particular society at a particular historical moment and our personal histories. The total freedom of the human condition provokes anguish but denying our freedom and refusing to accept responsibility for our actions is to act in **bad faith**. Similarly, if we deny our immanence, that is the givens of our situation, we also act in bad faith. (This is the central theme of Beauvoir's early short story cycle from the 1930s, *When Things of the Spirit Come First*.)

KEYWORDS

Essence: Characteristics which define human nature.

Project: What we choose to do in the world.

Authenticity: When we acknowledge our freedom and take responsibility for our actions.

For-itself: When we think of ourselves as transcendent consciousnesses, acknowledging our freedom and orienting ourselves towards things beyond ourselves.

In-itself: When we think of ourselves as things in the world, the givens of our situation.

Facticity: The givens of our situation.

Bad faith: When we deny our freedom and refuse to accept responsibility for our actions or when we deny the givens of our situation.

PHILOSOPHICAL FOUNDATIONS OF *THE SECOND SEX*

The Second Sex is founded in existentialism, but Beauvoir's ideas differ from Sartre's in a number of important ways. In *The Second Sex*, she starts from the notion that man poses himself as the **Subject**, as the essential, and that woman is defined in relation to man as the **Other** and associated with the inessential. As the Other, woman is doomed to immanence (non-transcendence). The tragedy of women's situation lies in the conflict between their fundamental aspirations as free and autonomous human beings and the fact that they live in a world where men compel them to be inessential, to be objects to their subject. Beauvoir defines this as oppression and argues that women who fail to act authentically as free human beings cannot necessarily be accused of being in bad faith. She rejects Sartre's concept of absolute freedom and choice, in favour of a concept of situated freedom, that is freedom that is relative and socially mediated. Beauvoir's approach, like Sartre's, can be traced back to a **phenomenological** perspective which views humans as situated beings who can only be understood within the total context of the complex world in which they live.

> **KEYWORDS**
>
> **Subject:** The essential, the sovereign.
>
> **Other:** The inessential, the subordinate.
>
> **Phenomenology:** The philosophical method that attempts to describe our experience directly.

JOY

Beauvoir's philosophical ideas are more optimistic than existentialists' generally, and leave more room for joy. In contrast to the view that anxiety, dread, fear and anguish necessarily result from the recognition of human freedom and non-self-identity and are part of the human condition, Beauvoir sees our responses as conditioned by our personal and social histories. Conceivably, the anguish of freedom may be a 'tension' that we actually desire and even embrace with joy (*The Ethics of Ambiguity*, p. 95). Beauvoir also highlights the joy to be had from disclosing being, that is from our awareness of the world revealing itself

As the other, woman is doomed to understand our existence in to our consciousness. Joy in human existence can also come from reciprocity, when individuals recognize each other as free subjects.

PHILOSOPHICAL ESSAYS

While it is true to say that Beauvoir developed her philosophical ideas in her fiction and elsewhere, she also wrote two book-length philosophical essays, *Pyrrhus et Cinéas* (1944), shortly to be available in English, and *The Ethics of Ambiguity* (1947), and, in addition, published two books of collected philosophical essays, *Existentialisme et la sagesse des nations* (1948), shortly to be available in English, and *Must We Burn De Sade?* (1955).

Pyrrhus et Cinéas is written as a dialogue between the two eponymous characters who have very different attitudes to life. The book, which popularized existentialism, reflects Beauvoir's efforts to define her moral and social responsibilities to others, arising from her experiences of the Nazi Occupation. Beauvoir wrote *The Ethics of Ambiguity* to counter arguments that existentialism can provide no basis for morality.

EVALUATION

Beauvoir herself was very severe when it came to evaluating her philosophical essays. *Pyrrhus et Cinéas* was too individualistic, she says, and failed to situate human projects and decisions in society (*The Prime of Life*, pp. 549–50). Its **idealism** robbed her speculations of almost all their significance. Of all Beauvoir's books, *The Ethics of Ambiguity* was the one that irritated her the most. Although she does not distance herself from all the ideas she expressed in it, she sums up the essay by saying that 'on the whole I went to a great deal of trouble to present inaccurately a problem to which I then offered a [hollow] solution' (*Force of Circumstance*, p. 76). The essays collected in *existentialisme et la sagesse des nations* are, for Beauvoir, blemished by

KEYWORDS

Idealism: A worldview that places special value on ideas and ideals.

idealism and lacking in solid arguments (*Force of Circumstance*, p. 77).

Some critics have shared Beauvoir's harsh assessment. Terms that have been used to describe her philosophical arguments include: flawed, unsatisfactory, disappointing, unconvincing, unsophisticated and morally bankrupt. Others have argued that Beauvoir is too severe on herself and have welcomed her philosophy as impressive, influential and profoundly liberational. They argue that the disparaging terms some have used to describe her philosophy are not the outcome of a serious, scholarly evaluation of her work, which is only now being undertaken. Clearly, an accurate evaluation must await the completion of these studies. However, history has already judged the importance of her contribution to the theoretical framework for the twentieth-century feminist movement.

In *The Second Sex*, Beauvoir picks up again a theme only touched on in *The Ethics of Ambiguity*, and applies her philosophical ideas to the total situation of women.

---

* * *SUMMARY* * *

- Beauvoir was passionate about philosophy.

- She developed her philosophical ideas in her fiction as well as in her formal philosophical writings.

- Beauvoir is philosophically far more original than is generally assumed.

- She was chiefly interested in metaphysics and ethics.

- As an existentialist, she was concerned about questions of freedom and responsibility.

---

3 *The Second Sex*

The Second Sex was published in French (*Le Deuxième Sexe*) in 1949 and was first available in English in 1953. For many, this is Beauvoir's best known work. It is largely as the writer of *The Second Sex* that she owes her reputation as a feminist, yet when she wrote it, she was not a feminist, nor did she consider her book to be; she saw it as a theoretical study or a philosophical essay. When she wrote *The Second Sex*, Beauvoir believed that the overthrow of capitalism would bring about the liberation of women and make them men's equals. Her aim in writing her study of women was to help her contemporaries to understand themselves and their situation. It is an ambitious study of women through the ages, originally published in two volumes, together, over a thousand pages long. It is difficult to categorize this interdisciplinary work which contains material drawn from philosophy, biology, psychology, psychoanalysis, physiology, history, sociology and literary criticism.

GENESIS

How did Beauvoir come to write this momentous book? Almost by chance, according to Beauvoir's autobiography; she wanted to write about herself and realized that the first question she would have to answer was what being a woman had meant to her. Once she began to look closely at the question, what she found was a revelation to her; the world was a masculine world. She was astonished that she had not until then noticed what had been staring her in the face. She became so interested in the question that she gave up the idea of writing about herself and would spend the next two years reading and writing about **women's condition**.

> **KEYWORD**
>
> Women's condition: Women's position in society.

STYLE AND TONE

Surprisingly, perhaps, for a 'philosophical essay', the tone of *The Second Sex* is far from neutral and it is written in a very personal style. This is true despite the fact that Beauvoir writes about women as 'they', seeming, to some, to distance herself from women and their fate. As well as using examples from literature and the sciences, Beauvoir frequently illustrates her ideas with examples and anecdotes to do with herself and her friends and acquaintances. Her text is highly **figurative** and by turns, can be passionate, humorous or sarcastic.

> **KEYWORD**
>
> Figurative: Language characterized by metaphor (one thing is described as being another thing) and other figures of speech, the opposite of literal.

RECEPTION

When the first volume of *The Second Sex* was published in June 1949, it sold well – 22,000 copies in the first week – and was well received. When in May, June and July of that year, chapters from the second volume ('Sexual Initiation', 'The Lesbian' and 'The Mother') were published in the journal, *Les Temps modernes*, scandal erupted. The second volume, published in its entirety in November, sold well but it provoked violent attacks. According to Beauvoir's memoirs, she was accused of stating the obvious, inventing, parodying, digressing, ranting and, especially, of indecency (*Force of Circumstance*, p. 196–97). Many of the attacks were personal and Beauvoir herself was vilified; among other things, she was accused of being unsatisfied, frigid, nymphomaniac and lesbian. The Left as well as the Right were critical of *The Second Sex*, which the Catholic Church placed on the 'Index', its list of censored books. As for ordinary women, many disapproved of Beauvoir's book or were frightened by it, but many others were helped by it; it enabled them to resist images of themselves which they found unacceptable and to realize that their difficulties were not due to a fault in them but to a general condition which they might fight to change.

Beauvoir was shocked by the attacks that her book provoked. She seems to have been unaware of the response that her radical ideas might receive. This is surprising to say the least. After all, she wrote *The Second Sex* in the post-war years when France was Catholic and conservative. The worst excesses of the war-time Vichy regime may have been abolished, but injustices persisted and at the end of the 1940s, pro-natalist policies created an atmosphere that was hostile to the sexual freedom of women who were expected to find fulfillment in marriage and motherhood. Abortion and contraception were illegal and women had no parental rights. In fact, it was not until 1965 that women could even open a bank account or have a job without their husband's permission.

It was in this context that Beauvoir set out to examine the total situation of women, in order to answer the philosophical question, 'what is a woman?' When it was first published in France, controversy stirred up by *The Second Sex* centered on Beauvoir's views on sexual difference and femininity, marriage and motherhood.

SEXUAL DIFFERENCE AND FEMININITY

Many of Beauvoir's early readers mistakenly believed that she denies the existence of sexual difference. In fact, her review of the biological differences between women and men leads her to describe women as the prey of the species in that they bear the burden of reproduction. However, although she sees biological considerations as a crucial element in women's situation, she denies that they determine women's fate and argues that they cannot justify or explain women's subordination.

The second volume of *The Second Sex* begins with Beauvoir's famous proposition: 'One is not born, but rather becomes, a woman'. She is making a distinction between sex and gender and asserting that there is no such thing as a feminine essence, a predetermined femininity, but that the way women are is the result of the situation in which they find themselves. Beauvoir finds evidence to support the radical idea that femininity is socially constructed in her analysis of the traditional destiny of women.

MARRIAGE

Beauvoir's views on marriage are very negative. She admits that by the late 1940s, the institution of marriage has been changed for the better by the improved economic situation of women who can now enjoy more freedom and more equality, but argues that in many ways it has not altered. Generally, marriage is still seen as the only acceptable destiny for women, most of whom are married, have been married, are about to be married or are suffering because they are not married. She describes in detail just how marriage mutilates women and dooms them to immanence to the extent that their lives become dominated by the perpetuation of the species and care of the home. For Beauvoir, marriage is an oppressive institution that demands great sacrifices of women.

Not least of these is sexual fulfillment. Much of Beauvoir's chapter on marriage is devoted to the impossibility of a happy sex life in marriage. She tells horror stories about women's experiences during their wedding nights when they are frequently shocked, frightened, humiliated and disappointed by their first sexual encounters. She goes as far as using the term 'obscene' to describe sex within marriage where it becomes a duty or a service rendered, rather than a free expression of spontaneous desire. To Beauvoir's mind, even though some couples may enjoy a fulfilling sexual relationship in the first years of marriage, erotic attraction is unlikely to last for long as couples come either to dislike or disgust one another or, alternatively, to be too familiar, too close to one another. Erotic fantasies may help, but these are, for Beauvoir, a very sad and dismal last resort. It is not that satisfying sex cannot exist for women – after all, Beauvoir, at the time she was writing *The Second Sex*, was involved in a passionate physical relationship with the American writer, Nelson Algren – but that it is dependent on the lovers' mutual recognition of their freedom and desire; something Beauvoir thinks unlikely to be found in marriage.

Beauvoir shocked her contemporaries with her devastating portrayal of married life. She subjects the ideal of happiness that marriage promises to women, to a biting analysis. The home, the physical embodiment of this ideal, becomes, she tells her readers, the centre of women's universe and they seek to turn their prison into an empire. Housework, women's way of appropriating their empire, is, however, a never-ending losing battle against dirt that Beauvoir likens to the torture of Sisyphus. Day after day, over and over, they wash dishes, dust furniture and mend clothes that tomorrow will be dirty, dusty and torn again. Housewives never have the sense that they have achieved a positive Good, but that they are engaged in a constant struggle against Evil. In their war against dust, stains, mud, dirt they are fighting sin, wrestling with Satan. Taken to its extreme, the quest for cleanliness and order can become pathological. Beauvoir describes women whose obsessive battle against dirt leads them to see life itself as a threat to their world because life means decomposition and more mess. Anyone entering their empire holds the threat of more thankless work: 'Wipe your feet; don't make a mess; don't touch.'

Housework: A pointless and constant struggle.

Cooking, Beauvoir tells us, can be more rewarding than cleaning. It is more creative. She writes about the pleasure to be had from shopping for ingredients and the opportunity this gives women to meet each other; she writes nostalgically about the 'magic' of fire and lyrically about the joy of making jam, bread, pastry and cakes. But the mood of the text changes abruptly; repeated day after day, cooking becomes just as boring and mechanical as cleaning. Only writers can afford to be poetic about housework because they never do any! The saddest thing of all for Beauvoir is that housework does not lead to the creation of anything that lasts. Women must constantly resist the temptation to see what they do as an end in itself and willingly see their work destroyed, the cake eaten, the polished floor walked on. The alternative is for mothers and housewives to turn into cruel shrews. Married life can take on many forms but the typical day of a housewife is characterized by boredom, waiting impatiently for husband and children to come home, and disappointment.

For Beauvoir's readers, trapped in unhappy marriages and failing to live up to the ideal, it was liberating to be told that individuals are not responsible for the failure of marriage. According to Beauvoir, it is the perverted institution of marriage as such, not the lack of good will on the part of individuals, that leads to dishonesty, conflict and meanness between married couples. Loyalty and friendship can only exist between husband and wife when they are both free and there is real equality in their relationship. To the extent that men alone possess economic independence and hold privileges associated with masculinity, they naturally appear tyrannical and women are driven to revolt and dissimulation. Even when couples do reach a compromise and manage to live together in relative harmony, the one curse they very rarely escape is boredom. After several months or years, they have nothing left to say to one another. Beauvoir's conclusion is bleak; at twenty, mistress of a home, bound permanently to one man and with a baby in her arms, a woman's life is over forever.

Yet Beauvoir does hold out hope for women. Fulfilling relationships with men are possible – more likely outside marriage than within – when they are based on individual autonomy and freedom. Beauvoir argues that economic independence for women and their working outside the home are of crucial importance. Both women and men will continue to be tormented and oppressed by the institution of marriage, despite the illusion of growing equality between the sexes, as long as women remain economically dependent on their husbands. Beauvoir wants to outlaw marriage as a career for women.

MOTHERHOOD

Although Beauvoir is bitterly ironic at the expense of idealized notions of motherhood, in fact, her views are far more positive than when she is discussing marriage.

The fact that this chapter of *The Second Sex* begins with a frank discussion of abortion, then illegal, shocked many of Beauvoir's contemporaries. Defying the taboo which made the topic unmentionable, she forthrightly exposes the hypocrisy surrounding it. She denounces the fact that because abortion is a criminal offence, each year, hundreds of women are forced either to undergo illegal, clandestine abortions in dangerous conditions or to go through with an unwanted pregnancy, pointing out that the society that is so keen to defend the rights of the embryo takes no interest in the well-being of these unwanted children once they are born. Beauvoir angrily dismisses the moral arguments of the Church and legal and practical arguments commonly made against abortion. She counterbalances these with the stories of real women who have had abortions, many of them with a number of children already. She relates horrifying stories of the dangerous lengths women go to provoke a miscarriage and avoid an unwanted pregnancy: self-abortion with a knitting needle; injecting vinegar in the uterus; drinking a cup of soap and running for a quarter of an hour; falling off a ladder or throwing themselves downstairs. She does not, however, underestimate the difficult moral choice that abortion represents to many women and the psychological and emotional trauma that can follow. She argues passionately in favour of contraception and legal abortion which would allow women to choose freely whether to have children or not.

Beauvoir shocked many people by arguing that there is no such thing as a maternal 'instinct'. She shows that it is the total situation in which women find themselves that determines whether a baby represents a burden or a treasure. She voices the rarely heard fears and uncertainties, regrets and even hostility, that can coexist with the amazed curiosity and joy of a new mother. But, she argues, unless circumstances are positively unfavourable, women's lives are enriched by children. She applauds the generosity of mothers. What she objects to is the idealization of mothers; pure maternal devotion can exist but, ordinarily, motherhood is a strange compromise of narcissism, altruism, dreams, sincerity, bad-faith, devotion and cynicism. All mothers are not exemplary; bad mothers exist.

Beauvoir's lengthy portrayal of cruel, tyrannical, sadistic mothers made uncomfortable reading for many of her contemporaries. As she pointed out, it is not that such mothers were unheard of but that the idea tends to be hypocritically projected onto the character of the 'cruel stepmother'. The danger, as Beauvoir sees it, is that in a majority of cases, helpless children are dependent on unhappy, unsatisfied women.

Although Beauvoir rejects the common assumptions that motherhood necessarily leads to fulfillment for women (there are plenty of unhappy, bitter, unsatisfied mothers) and that children are necessarily happy in their mother's arms, she is not denying that good mothers do exist. She argues that motherhood only leads to fulfillment if it is sincerely and freely chosen. Only well-balanced, healthy women, in a position psychologically, morally and materially to meet the needs of a child and aware of their responsibilities, can become 'good mothers' who genuinely and selflessly desire the happiness of their children. Motherhood is a valid project for women but, like all projects, it has no intrinsic justification. In Beauvoir's opinion, having children should not be seen as something natural but as a moral choice that carries with it a commitment.

Beauvoir argues that women who are whole human beings make better mothers. She is absolutely in favour of mothers working outside the home; women who lead full and satisfying lives have more to give to their children and make fewer demands of them. In a passage that might still be written today, more than fifty years after the publication of *The Second Sex*, Beauvoir deplores the fact that all too often it is difficult to reconcile bringing up children with having a job. She lays the blame firmly on the kind of jobs women do (many of them like slavery) and the lack of adequate childcare. Typically fearless, Beauvoir asserts that children are, in any case, better off if they spend less time with their parents and more in the care of other adults.

BEAUVOIR'S UTOPIA

Beauvoir's conclusion provides her readers with an optimistic vision of a future in which women are free, autonomous human beings. It is a powerful and inspiring utopia. Beauvoir shows how freedom and equality would transform all aspects of women's lives. *The Second Sex* is a liberating book because it demonstrates that the way things are is not necessarily the way things have to be. Beauvoir ends with a call for freedom, and for women and men to affirm their fellowship (brotherhood) in order to achieve this supreme victory.

CONCLUSION

The Second Sex did not have an immediate political or intellectual impact, other than on a personal level for individual readers. Later, in the 1970s, a generation of emerging feminists read *The Second Sex* and were inspired by it. Many of Beauvoir's analyses, such as the distinction between sex and gender, have since been developed in radical directions.

The Second Sex offers women a powerful vision of freedom and change. For many, it has represented a lifeline which has helped them to make sense of their lives. For many years, Beauvoir received letters from women of all ages and all walks of life, thanking her for her book. Countless feminist theorists have been influenced by Beauvoir's monumental book which reframed the whole question of women's oppression. For Beauvoir herself, *The Second Sex* was, she wrote, the work which possibly brought her the greatest satisfaction (*Force of Circumstances*, p. 202).

POSTSCRIPT: READING *THE SECOND SEX*

The Second Sex is not an easy book to read. It is very long and repetitious. Beauvoir hammers home her points with multiple examples. She said herself that if she were to have rewritten her book in the 1960s, she would have made it shorter and more streamlined. Reading *The Second Sex* in translation brings with it an additional set of problems. The translator has cut the original extensively, deleting, for example, much of the section on housework. It is also the case that the translation is frequently clumsy and mistranslations mean that certain passages in English are at best misleading, at worst incomprehensible. Unfortunately, this is particularly true of the philosophical terminology Beauvoir uses.

* * * SUMMARY * * *

- *The Second Sex* (1949) was written as a philosophical essay. It is a study of the total situation of women.

- It is an interdisciplinary work which contains material drawn from philosophy, biology, psychology, psychoanalysis, physiology, history, sociology and literary criticism.

- *The Second Sex* was an extremely controversial book, particularly because of Beauvoir's views on sexual difference and femininity, marriage and motherhood.

- Beauvoir argues that the biological differences between women and men cannot justify or explain the subordination of women.

- She demonstrates that femininity is socially constructed: 'One is not born, but rather becomes, a woman.'

- She argues that marriage is a perverted institution.

- She denies the existence of maternal instinct.

- Beauvoir offers women a utopian vision of how their lives might be transformed by freedom and equality.

4 Early Fiction

Aged 16, Beauvoir set her heart on becoming a famous author who, by writing about her own experience, would justify her existence and would earn 'the undying love of millions of hearts' (*Memoirs of a Dutiful Daughter*, p. 142). In fact, the writing of fiction did not come easily to Beauvoir. It was not until 1943 that her first novel, *She Came to Stay* was published. Her early attempts at writing had ended in failure. Between 1929 and 1935, she began and abandoned a number of novels, unhappy with the way she had tried to transpose her own experience into fiction. In 1935, she began work on *When Things of the Spirit Come First*, a collection of five, loosely connected short stories. These were completed in 1937 but rejected by two publishers, Gallimard and Grasset. Seemingly, this was not because they were badly written but because the subject matter – the lives of young, middle-class women – was deemed to be subversive and unpublishable at that time. Beauvoir would actually decide to publish them in 1979.

SHE CAME TO STAY

Beauvoir started work on *She Came to Stay* in October 1938. In her memoirs, she writes that 'literature is born when something in life goes slightly adrift' (*The Prime of Life*, p. 365). Only when her happiness was threatened by the Olga-Sartre-Beauvoir 'trio' did she find she had 'something to say'.

She Came to Stay transposes the unhappy experience of the 'trio' into fiction. It tells the story of the heroine, Françoise Miquel's emotional and metaphysical crisis and of how her apparently strong relationship with Pierre Labrousse, a well-known actor and producer, is shaken when Xavière Pagès is invited to come and share their life in Paris. It can be read as an account of Françoise's struggle to selfhood.

The historical context of the story – the outbreak of war – is understated for the greater part of the narrative and the main focus is the characters' feelings. Because of this, the claustrophobic atmosphere is intensified and the characters appear all the more trapped in their obsessions. Tensions arise when Xavière is far less submissive than the older couple wishes and refuses to allow herself to be annexed by them. Xavière wants more than Françoise is prepared to give and, moreover, seeks to establish a relationship with Pierre, independently of her. Françoise begins to question her relationship with Pierre when he appears to take Xavière more seriously than she does and she is forced to accept they are two separate people and to recognize her overdependence on him.

It is not simple sexual jealousy that brings about Françoise's crisis when Pierre decides to seduce Xavière. Her relationship with Pierre has never been monogamous. The epigraph from the philosopher, Hegel – 'Each consciousness pursues the death of the other' – (unfortunately omitted from the English translation), directs readers to a philosophical/ metaphysical interpretation of the triangular relationship. Xavière, a hostile consciousness, represents a threat to Françoise's very sense of self. Clearly, psychological interpretations are also possible. The 'trio' can be seen to be playing out a quasi-oedipal drama where the adolescent girl competes with the mother for the father's attention – it is interesting that Beauvoir gave Françoise her own mother's name. Although Françoise, who is ill at ease with her own femininity, wishes to see Xavière as a child, she is nevertheless forced to recognize that the adolescent Xavière is on the threshold of womanhood. An intense emotional conflict with powerful sexual overtones builds up between the two women. Françoise's maternal feelings for Xavière are overlain with sexual, and thus quasi-incestuous desire. Her physical response to Xavière and her desire to possess her have unmistakable lesbian connotations.

A number of events move the narrative towards its violent climax. In a stereotypically masculine way, Pierre, mad with jealousy when Xavière takes Gerbert as a lover, loses interest in her when she is loving towards him and at his disposal. He ends their affair, supposedly reluctantly, by encouraging Xavière to focus fully on her relationship with Gerbert. His plan is upset somewhat because Françoise, in a move of self-affirmation, has meanwhile begun an affair with Gerbert herself. Françoise and Pierre agree to keep Xavière in ignorance, partly out of fear that she may commit suicide but also, on Françoise's part, out of malice. She is happy to allot Xavière 'a daily ration of soothing lies' as 'scorned, duped, she would no longer dispute Françoise's place in the world' (p. 378).

The final chapter takes place after the outbreak of war when Pierre and Gerbert are at the Front. By this stage, Xavière's childish hostility towards Françoise has become a 'true female hatred' (p. 392). One day, Xavière takes the key to Françoise's desk, reads her letters and discovers Pierre's scornful feelings for her and Gerbert's deceit and betrayal. Françoise's triumph is reversed; Xavière's interpretation of events is very different from hers: 'You were jealous of me because Labrousse was in love with me. You made him loathe me and to get better revenge, you took Gerbert from me (p.405).' Françoise murders Xavière to wipe out this view of herself, to wrest narrative control back from Xavière and tell her own version of the story. Metaphysically speaking, she asserts her sovereignty and defeats a hostile consciousness. Of course, on another level, she defeats her rival and keeps the love of both men. Françoise also sees the murder as a way for her to assert her independence from Pierre; she has acted alone.

Beauvoir disliked the ending she gave to her first novel for artistic reasons – she found it clumsy and implausible – but she says, it was 'the motive force and raison d'être behind the entire novel' (*The Prime of Life*, p. 340). The murder was in fact 'cathartic' for her. Not only did it allow her to put the failed 'trio' behind her, she also regained her personal autonomy through her identification with her heroine and her violent act of self-affirmation.

Narrative techniques

The **story** is told in the third person (he/she) by an external narrator (someone who is not a character in the story). However, this narrator is not **omniscient** and remains fairly covert or hidden. This is in line with Beauvoir's moral and metaphysical stance; she wished her characters to appear to be free beings, responsible for their own destinies. The narration is always focused through one of the characters and only ever relates what is within the consciousness of the character acting as **focalizer**. Readers have direct access to characters' voices as much of the **narrative** is made up of dialogues between the main protagonists who are preoccupied with the meaning of each other's words and actions. For Beauvoir, dialogue is a form of action, it moves the story forward.

KEYWORDS

Story: A succession of events.

Omniscient: With total, God-like knowledge of the characters and their actions.

Focalizer: The character through whose perspective the story is presented.

Narrative: The process of production of a text.

Text: The discourse that tells a story.

The story is mainly viewed through the eyes of Françoise, the Beauvoir figure ($14^{1}/_{2}$ chapters out of 18). Brief shifts of focus to Elisabeth, Pierre's sister, and to Gerbert allow Françoise to be seen from the outside and also enable readers to judge the trustworthiness or otherwise of her perceptions. In fact both Elisabeth's and Gerbert's narratives tend to support Françoise's views. It is very significant that Xavière – demonized in the **text** – is denied a voice and readers never hear her side of the story.

Writing practice

It is frequently assumed by critics that Beauvoir paid little attention to the style of her novels. In fact, Beauvoir attached a great deal of importance to the artistic reworking of lived experience and to the creative process. In interviews she gave, she was categorical that style, the craft of writing, had always mattered a great deal to her. In *Force of*

Circumstance she describes the long, painstaking process of reworking the drafts of her books. In her contribution to a 1964 debate, *Que peut la littérature* (What can literature do?), Beauvoir is categorical that in literature, which is essentially a process of discovery for author and readers alike, the distinction between style and content is obsolete and that the two are inseparable.

She Came to Stay is a highly figurative text. One of the most striking things about it is Beauvoir's use of excessive, hyperbolic, extravagant language. Beauvoir's writing is more likely to evoke emotion and work on readers' feelings than it is to prompt an intellectual response or rational argument. Highly coloured, extravagant passages occur at climactic points in the narrative. The language is excessive because it has come up against the inexpressible. What is threatening Françoise is beyond language, beyond thought even:

> Behind [Xavière's] maniacal grin, was the threat of a danger more positive than any she had ever imagined. Something was there that hungrily hugged itself, that unquestionably existed on its own account. Approach to it was impossible even in thought. Just as she seemed to be getting near it the thought dissolved. This was no tangible object, but an incessant flux, a never ending flight, only comprehensible to itself, and forever occult.
>
> *(She Came to Stay*, p. 285 tr. adap.)

This writing relies on hyperbole for its impact.

Reception

When *She Came to Stay* was published in France during the Occupation, in 1943, it met with enormous success: reviews were favourable and sales were good. At the age of 35, Beauvoir became a major intellectual figure in her own right.

In writing *She Came to Stay*, Beauvoir found her voice and it seemed to her that, in future, she would always have something to say.

THE MANDARINS

Beauvoir's second and third novels, *The Blood of Others* and *All Men are Mortal* belong to what has been called her 'moral period'. Beauvoir waited until 1949 to begin work on her fourth novel, *The Mandarins*. At the heart of the novel is the story of her love affair with Nelson Algren that she was reluctant to expose to 'a harsh and jealous world'. The novel also deals with French politics since the Liberation – 'the feverish and disappointing story of what happened after the war' (*Force of Circumstance*, p. 201). Beauvoir is interested in the role of intellectuals in politics and the relationship between morality and political action.

The slightly ironic title, *The Mandarins*, refers to intellectuals. The term's pejorative edge means readers cannot be absolutely sure what attitude to adopt with regard to their status and influence, although in interviews Beauvoir said she intended the irony to be mild and sympathetic.

The Mandarins is Beauvoir's longest and most complex book. It is also a very personal book. She tells us in her memoirs that she put all of herself in it. A great deal of autobiographical material is used in her detailed evocation of the period 1944–48. Events contemporaneous with the writing of the novel had an impact on it, too. All the important issues and events in the novel are true: the first atomic bomb, the Cold War, the Soviet labour camps, the purge. Beauvoir portrays intellectuals facing difficult moral choices; she wanted to depict the times without claiming to provide any answers. She was impatient with those who saw her book as merely a *roman à clef*.

KEYWORD

Roman à clef: A novel in which the characters are thinly disguised representations of real people.

For Beauvoir, the central theme of her novel is the break-up and rebuilding of a friendship; the friends concerned are writers, Robert Dubreuilh and Henri Perron. The story of the quarrel is told from two viewpoints: Henri's own and Robert's partner, well-known psychiatrist, Anne Dubreuilh's. However, the novel is far more wide-ranging than this might imply. It follows Henri and Anne and those close to them as they struggle with the complexities of their personal relationships and political commitments in the post-Liberation years. Themes developed in *The Mandarins* include:

* individual morality

* the function and value of literature

* the philosophical and moral significance of psychiatry/psychotherapy

* the nature of love, including the plight of women who make a cult of love

* heterosexual relationships

* women's sexuality

* mother–daughter relationships

* women's condition and the social construction of gender.

The key value in the novel is the notion of preference which is founded on 'repetition' in the Kierkegaardian sense. According to the philosopher Kierkegaard, to possess something fully we must have lost and then found it again. During the course of the novel, Henri and Dubreuilh abandon their friendship, their writing and political action, with their optimistic idealism utterly betrayed. At the end of the novel, they return to where they started from, now fully aware of the difficulties, compromises and failures that friendship, literary work and political action imply. Their old idealistic convictions have been replaced by stark preferences.

The same pattern of preference is played out in personal relationships too. At the beginning of the novel, Anne is fully committed to her relationship with Robert, with whom she identifies completely. On a trip to the United States, she begins a passionate love affair with Lewis Brogan. Anne has to choose. On the one hand, Robert represents safety, companionship, a shared life, values in common. On the other, Lewis, who loves and needs her absolutely, offers sexual passion and fidelity. Anne is a romantic but recognizes that 'love isn't everything' (*The Mandarins*, p. 574). Anne first decides to stay with Robert. When she changes her mind and decides to go to Lewis after all, on condition that he sends for her, the letter she is hoping for does not come and she lacks the courage to leave her life in France. She is brought to the brink of suicide before enacting the pattern of preference by choosing life and her relationship with Robert over the absolutes of love and death.

Narrative techniques

The narrative is divided, roughly equally, between the points of view of Anne and Henri. Their narratives alternate throughout the novel as they each in turn respond to what is happening in their lives and in the world. Beauvoir intended the two narratives to undercut and correct each other, but in fact they tend to complement one another instead. This is not to deny the very real differences between Anne and Henri's perspectives. These are largely due to the way in which Beauvoir divides her autobiographical traits between the two characters, strictly and – unfortunately, one might add – according to gender stereotypes, with Henri possessing the positive aspects of Beauvoir's experience and Anne the negative.

Henri is characterized by:

* a taste for activity

* optimism

* enthusiasm for life

* a desire to change the world

* writing.

Anne is defined in terms of her:

* passivity

* fear

* shame

* preoccupation with death

* dependence.

One important difference between the two narratives is that whereas Henri's point of view is narrated in the third person by an external narrator, Anne narrates her own story in the first person. She is the first female character in Beauvoir's fiction to do so. Much of her narrative is retrospective, but it begins and ends as a monologue in the present tense where her experiencing and narrating selves coincide. For the first time in Beauvoir's fiction, readers hear directly the female voice of suffering and madness that will dominate her later fiction.

From a feminist perspective, *The Mandarins* is problematical for a number of reasons. It is not only that there are no 'positive heroines' in the novel – a point that Beauvoir acknowledged 'unrepentantly' (*Force of Circumstance*, p. 278). There is also:

* the negative portrayal of female sexuality as grotesque and obscene (muted to some extent in the English translation)

* the indulgent treatment of sexist, masculinist attitudes which Beauvoir possibly did not even recognize as sexist at the time she was writing.

The Mandarins is considered by many to be Beauvoir's best work. When it was published in 1954, Beauvoir was awarded France's most prestigious literary prize, the *Goncourt.* She was delighted with the good reviews and the admiring letters she received from her readers. Her childhood dream of being loved through her books had come true!

* * *SUMMARY* * *

● Beauvoir published her first novel, *She Came to Stay*, in 1943. It transposes into fiction the triangular relationship between Beauvoir, Sartre and Olga. It explores the problem of the existence of other consciousnesses.

● *The Mandarins* (1954) focuses on the lives of intellectuals after the Liberation and asks questions about politics and morality. A fictionalized account of Beauvoir's love affair with Nelson Algren is at the heart of the novel. It was awarded France's most prestigious literary prize, the *Goncourt.*

● Beauvoir attached a great deal of importance to the style of her books and believed that there was no distinction between style and content.

Later Fiction 5

When Simone de Beauvoir took up writing fiction again in 1966, she did so in a very different context and her technique and style were very different, too. Since the publication of *The Mandarins* in 1954, her autobiography and the autobiographical account of her mother's death, *A Very Easy Death*, had been the main focus of her writing. Why did she turn to writing fiction again?

* Instead of writing about herself, Beauvoir wanted to think about themes not directly to do with her own experience and characters with lives very different from her own.

* The literary context. In the 1950s and 1960s, the **New Novelists** were engaged in a radical rethinking of the novel form. Beauvoir had turned to autobiography, partly out of misgivings to do with the novel form and although she was by no means a partisan of the **New Novel**, she did share some of the New Novelists' criticisms of the traditional novel. By 1966, the debate had made it possible to write very different novels.

KEYWORDS

New Novel / New Novelists: The French writer Alain Robbe-Grillet led debate about the New Novel (*nouveau roman*) in the 1950s and 1960s. In his avant-garde, experimental anti-novels, traditional characteristics of the novel such as plot, characterization and narrative were rejected.

* Her new relationship with Sylvie le Bon provided emotional stability.

Although the novel *Les Belles Images* (1966) and short story collection *The Woman Destroyed* (1968) focus on the lives of women, and although the narrative voice in these texts belongs to women, it is important to bear in mind that neither book was intended to be a feminist work as such. Beauvoir's women protagonists are not feminist heroines who provide us with positive role models. Beauvoir was hurt when some feminists reacted with hostility to her work and accused her of betrayal, but she rejected their criticism: 'I really do not feel obliged to choose exemplary heroines. It does not seem to me that describing failure, error and bad faith means betraying anyone at all' (*All Said and Done*, p. 144). Beauvoir is representing women as they are, not as they have to be or might be.

In her contribution to the 1964 debate, *Que peut la littérature?*, Beauvoir's argument is that to reveal the world is to act on it and so to change it. She believes that literature can help us overcome our separation from one another by revealing that what is most personal to us is shared by others. Beauvoir believes that 'failure, outrages, death, must be spoken of, not to make readers despair, but, on the contrary, to try to save them from despair' (p. 92 author's translation). Many of Beauvoir's readers wrote to tell her they agreed and that Laurence's story was theirs: 'Yes, that is exactly our story; that is just the world we live in; and like Laurence we too feel imprisoned, caught in a trap' (*All Said and Done*, p. 138). When the title story, 'The Woman Destroyed', appeared in instalments in *Elle* magazine, Beauvoir was inundated with letters from women identifying with the main protagonist, Monique. Recognizing their own plight in Beauvoir's fiction, readers were better able to act to change their situation.

LES BELLES IMAGES

Les Belles Images is the shortest of Beauvoir's novels and was the fastest and easiest to write. It is also the the most literary. The ironic title (untranslated in the English version) means 'pretty pictures'. It can be understood on a number of levels, evoking not only the advertising images that the main female protagonist, Laurence, manipulates in her job in advertising, but also the glossy veneer of the consumer society that hides injustice and oppression.

The novel is a bitter attack on the technocratic middle class and its blind optimism in the future. Beauvoir allowed the **technocrats** to 'speak for themselves' by collecting examples of their phraseology and formulas in the media and incorporating them in her text. Beauvoir highlights the ideological function of language which is used to shore up cherished myths – frequently to comic effect.

> **KEYWORD**
>
> Technocrat: A scientist, engineer, or other expert who is one of a group of similar people who have political power as well as technical knowledge.

Technique

For the first time in Beauvoir's fiction, no character speaks for her. Readers see the world through the eyes of Laurence, a young wife and mother with a full-time career as an advertising copywriter. The technical challenge for Beauvoir was to make the silence speak, to get readers to read between the lines: 'The difficulty lay in making the ugliness of the world that stifles her, show through her plight, without intervening myself' (*All Said and Done*, p. 138 tr. adap.).

Laurence's plight

Laurence is very much a product of the technocratic middle class. In fact, in terms of the codes by which they live, she is a supreme performer, socially accomplished and a skilled manipulator of images. Ostensibly, she has everything to make her happy: an attentive husband in Jean-Charles, two lovely daughters, a lover, a career, a nice home and plenty of money. Yet, she is deeply uneasy and alienated from those around her. Laurence is painfully aware of her separateness; the words, 'what have the others got that I haven't?' (p. 23), echo in the text. For Laurence, 'the world is everywhere somewhere else, and there's no way of getting in' (p. 32 tr. adap.). Her subjectivity is fragile and she searches constantly for a sense of who she is, a sense of identity. She has already suffered a breakdown and recognizes her vulnerability.

The reality of tragedy and unhappiness in the world intrudes in her life and threatens to destabilize her again when her elder daughter,

Catherine, is upset by a poster of a starving child in Africa. Laurence cannot answer her questions: 'Why do we exist?' 'Why isn't everybody given enough to eat?' When consoling lies do not work, the reaction of Jean-Charles, supported by other members of the family, is to send Catherine to a psychologist to cure her of her sadness and, in the meantime, to put an end to her friendship with Brigitte, a slightly older, more worldly child, whom they blame for upsetting Catherine and lowering her marks at school. Laurence is appalled. Her crisis is exacerbated by the profound disappointment she feels over her father.

Laurence recognizes her powerlessness, and her inner conflict and pain are manifested in her body. She is unable to eat and her rejection of food comes to stand for her rejection of her world and her self: 'What have they turned me into? This woman who loves no one, indifferent to the beauties of the world, incapable even of crying, this woman that I'm vomiting up' (p. 219 tr. adap.). For Laurence, her refusal to eat is an expression of her revolt. She has found the strength to refuse to bring up Catherine the same way she was brought up, and tells Jean-Charles that 'bringing up a child doesn't mean making them into a pretty picture…' (p. 220 tr. adap.). Through identifying with her daughter and wanting to defend her, Laurence begins to challenge, in a limited way, the values of her class.

Narrative strategies

In *Les Belles Images*, Laurence is always the focalizer, but the narrative voice is divided between the first and third persons. The way the narrative voice shifts from 'I' to 'she', not only from paragraph to paragraph but also within paragraphs and even within sentences, duplicates, on a textual level, Laurence's loss of psychic unity and feelings of alienation. In the early chapters, it is the third-person voice which dominates and the first-person which intrudes, interposing questions and comments. By the final chapter, the balance has shifted. Here, as Laurence struggles to understand what is happening to her, the first-person narrative is much stronger, more sustained and it is the third-person narrative that appears to intrude. 'She' erupts in the the most painful moments of Laurence's story. As her anguish reaches its climax, 'I' and 'she' alternate in the text:

> I'm jealous but above all, above all… She's breathing too fast, she's panting. […] The secret she blamed herself for not being able to find out, perhaps after all it didn't exist. It didn't exist. She has known since the trip to Greece. I was *disappointed.* The word stabs her. She presses her handkerchief against her teeth as though to hold back the cry she is incapable of uttering. I am disappointed. I have cause to be.
>
> (*Les Belles Images*, pp. 217–18 tr. adap.)

Laurence wins the battle with Jean-Charles over Catherine, but the lapse into the third person in the final paragraph mitigates any optimism over her own future.

Writing practice

The most striking thing about the text of *Les Belles Images*, is the way it is disrupted and fragmented. Just as Laurence's personality disintegrates, so too does the text. Multi-layering is sometimes very funny in *Les Belles Images*. At other times, it reproduces Laurence's inner conflict on a textual level. Beauvoir also uses broken, disarticulated syntax to convey Laurence's pain and anguish. Unfortunately the existing English translation does not always do justice to the rich complexity of Beauvoir's text.

THE WOMAN DESTROYED

Beauvoir wrote the short fiction collected in *The Woman Destroyed* in 1967. Three stories make up the collection:

* 'The Age of Discretion'

* 'The Monologue'

* 'The Woman Destroyed'.

All three stories are based on the lived experience of women in their forties who had written to Beauvoir about the break-up of their marriages and who ended up no longer knowing who they were. The themes of isolation and failure run through all the stories. As she portrays the plight of her women protagonists, Beauvoir also picks up again the themes of old age and motherhood, touched on in *Les Belles Images*. She adopts the same oblique technique she used in *Les Belles Images*, and asks her readers to read between the lines again. For Beauvoir, all the women are deceiving themselves and she is effectively asking her readers to spot the omissions, contradictions and falsehoods in their narratives, to track down the women as if they were tracking down the guilty character in a detective story, as Beauvoir said of 'The Woman Destroyed'.

'The Age of Discretion'

The unnamed central character in 'The Age of Discretion' is a self-deluded intellectual in her sixties whose best work is behind her. The story focuses on the conflict between the woman and her husband, André. They disagree over what it means to grow old and over their son, Philippe, who has decided to give up his academic career for a job in the Ministry of Culture that his father-in-law has found for him. The woman is disappointed in him for what she sees as a betrayal of principles that she cherishes and that she had thought were important to him too. Gradually, the discrepancies between the woman's beliefs and reality emerge. She replaces her idealized vision of old age with a bleak view of ageing as mental and physical decay – equally extreme, it should be noted. She also accepts that she can no longer dominate her son's life. She is shown more authorial understanding than the protagonists in the other stories; she begins to admit her mistakes and some hope is held out for her at the end as the couple is reconciled, dialogue is renewed and they face the future together.

The narrative is in the first-person and Beauvoir thought it the least satisfactory of the three tales, for its lack of silences and ambiguity.

'The Monologue'

Murielle, the central character in 'The Monologue', is a bitter and tyrannical woman on the brink of madness. The narrative takes place on New Year's Eve. Readers gradually piece together Murielle's story. Left by her first, unfaithful husband, Albert, she has driven her daughter, Sylvie, to suicide and has been abandoned by her second husband, Tristan, who has custody of their son, Francis. Murielle wants to persuade Tristan that they should live together again and goes over the case she is going to put to him when he visits her the following day. Her monologue is her self-justification, an attempt to construct a positive image of herself as the best mother in the world. Also, as the epigraph from Flaubert suggests, 'the monologue is her form of revenge' – it is a violent and extremely crude diatribe against all those who have committed real or imagined wrongs against her. Murielle is obsessed with sex; her monologue returns again and again to images of sex which is inevitably linked to dirt, perversion and disgust. Murielle's pain, anguish, desperation and rage are constantly in evidence.

As the title and epigraph of this story imply, the narrative is an interior monologue which reproduces the flow of consciousness in Murielle's mind. An associative logic carries the narrative forward – incidents are related in disorder, prompted by seemingly inconsequential details. Readers are drawn into Murielle's madness and obsession as they attempt to make sense of her monologue at the same time as they are repelled by the vulgarity and sordidness of her delusion.

'The Woman Destroyed'

Monique, the main protagonist in 'The Woman Destroyed', has devoted her life to being a wife and mother. Now, aged 44, after 22 years of marriage when both her daughters have left home, her husband, Maurice, reveals he has been having an affair with a younger, ambitious, career woman. Monique has defined herself through her husband and when Maurice leaves her, she loses her sense of self. She is forced to see that she has not been a perfect wife and mother. One by one, her illusions are shattered. As her crisis deepens, Monique, like Laurence, suffers from loss of appetite. Her weight loss is emblematic of her suffering. More foregrounded in the text is Monique's constant bleeding that lasts some 23 days. It is a metaphor for her loss of self, analogous to Laurence's vomiting. By the end of the story, Monique faces a frightening future alone.

'The Woman Destroyed' is written in diary form. To begin with, Monique uses her diary to allay her fears and deny the truth. When this proves impossible and as she loses her sense of self, Monique writes her diary in order to forge an identity, to discover who she is. Aware that her diary is not a repository of absolute truth, she continues to keep it all the same, as the process of writing reassures her she is still alive.

Writing practice

Beauvoir's writing practice means her texts are often demanding and uncomfortable. In *The Woman Destroyed*, Beauvoir's texts duplicate the disintegration of the sense of self experienced by the central characters and textual fragmentation and interruptions are conspicuous.

All three texts refuse to convey a sense of chronology, a sense of linear logic. This is particularly marked in 'The Monologue', where present, past and future jostle in the text and the extremely convoluted narrative presents readers with a baffling, disordered series of statements. Although it is far from being as disrupted as 'The Monologue', 'The Woman Destroyed' is not a simple linear/chronological narrative either. The past disrupts the present to a lesser, though nonetheless real degree as memories involuntarily erupt into Monique's thoughts.

Disruptive syntax is characteristic of *The Woman Destroyed*. 'The Monologue' is Beauvoir's most transgressive text and her most 'crazy'. This is largely due to its eccentric syntax. The text is not without punctuation but conventional rules of punctuation are flouted. A sense of disarray is generated as readers, largely deprived of boundaries normally marked by punctuation, attempt to make sense of the text. In places, disarticulated, disjointed, convulsive syntax is used to translate Murielle's distress.

THE VOICE OF PAIN AND MADNESS

Beauvoir's later fiction is written from a single viewpoint and only women's voices are heard. It seems natural that her autobiographical writing should have prompted her to write more self-consciously as a woman and so make women more prominent in the later fiction. As women have moved to the foreground, there has been a concomitant loss in narrative authority – readers cannot trust Laurence, the woman, Murielle, or Monique. The texts focus on the misuse of language to hide the truth and create myths. Significantly, the narrative voice in the later fiction has become a voice of pain and madness. 'Negative women' are nothing new in Beauvoir's fiction – in every novel, failed artists and women on the brink of madness form the shadow sides of the more positive character-narrator female figures, who are themselves threatened with madness. What is new in *Les Belles Images* and *The Woman Destroyed* is that 'negative women' now occupy centre stage and narrate their own stories. It has been suggested that the presence of 'negative women' in fiction written by women, is linked to the anxiety of authorship of women writing in a masculine tradition. Various aspects of Beauvoir's fiction suggest she shared this anxiety.

RECEPTION

Both *Les Belles Images* and *The Woman Destroyed* were bestsellers. Hundreds of thousands of copies of the books were sold and the appearance of 'The Woman Destroyed' in instalments in *Elle*, before publication of the collection of three stories, brought Beauvoir many new readers. Many wrote appreciative letters to her. However, the later fiction was so different from what Beauvoir had written before, that the reaction of a number of readers and critics was that these were not 'real Simone de Beauvoir', as if they had somehow been cheated of a genuine product – ending up with a trivial 'shop-girl's romance' instead. Beauvoir was bitterly disappointed by the number of negative reviews.

Beauvoir was also disappointed because she felt her books had been misunderstood by many of her readers who, for example, identified with Monique and shared her blindness. Why do readers consistently 'misread' Beauvoir's books in this way? It has been shown that her **rhetorical strategies** sometimes undermine her intentions.

KEYWORD

Rhetorical strategies: The ways in which writers choose to communicate their message.

* * * SUMMARY * * *

- The fiction Beauvoir wrote in the 1960s was very different from her earlier fiction in terms of length, technique and style, themes, and autobiographical content.

- *Les Belles Images* (1966) is considered to be Beauvoir's most literary novel. It is a bitter attack on the technocratic middle class. It focuses on the emotional crisis of the main protaginist, Laurence.

- The three short stories collected in *The Woman Destroyed* (1967) examine the plight of women in their forties who, faced with the break-up of their marriages, and the prospect of old age, have no clear sense of who they are.

- Women are in the foreground in the later fiction and the narrative voice belongs exclusively to them.

- *Les Belles Images* and *The Woman Destroyed* were both bestsellers.

Autobiographical Writings

Beauvoir's impulse to write about herself was a constant from an early age. Critics have commented on the strong autobiographical current in all her writing. Of course, what makes the four volumes of memoirs she wrote distinct from her fiction and her philosophical essays is that, in them, she speaks in her own name. Beauvoir's wartime diaries and letters, published posthumously in 1990, and the letters she wrote to Algren, published in 1997, also contribute to the views we have of her life and times. The memoirs, bestsellers in France, have been among her most popular books and have always attracted her a wide readership.

WHY AUTOBIOGRAPHY?

Beauvoir frequently discusses her autobiographical project, in her memoirs themselves as well as in interviews and in a lecture she gave in Japan in 1966. In part, Beauvoir turned to autobiography because she was dissatisfied with the limitations of the novel form. She believes that the portrait of an individual life is, at the same time, a portrait of that person's milieu and era. She emphasizes the universal dimension of her memoirs, insisting that the account of her existence can throw light on the existence of others; she is speaking as a woman and for her century.

Testimony

Beauvoir believes that autobiography has an ethical dimension. She wrote her memoirs to bear witness to the intellectual, artistic, political and social life of her time. She saw this as a way of bringing about change. For testimony to be effective, it does not have to be impartial; Beauvoir's record of the major events in the twentieth century – the Holocaust, Hiroshima, the Cold War, the Algerian war, May 1968 and Feminism, to name but a few – is firmly rooted in her own personal experience. Some have questioned Beauvoir's testimonial authority in view of the fact that she did not actively participate in all the events she describes, but it seems reasonable to argue that the point of view of an observer of events is perfectly valid.

Writing the self

Beauvoir's intention was also to record and relate her life, in a sense to preserve her past selves, and to discover the meaning of her existence. She believes that her past exists as such only in so far as she narrates it – it is a narrative construct. Similarly, her self is constructed by the narrative; the figure we know today as 'Simone de Beauvoir' is not a real person but is, in part, the product of Beauvoir's text. The memoirs do not reveal a pre-existing real self which underlies the text (this is sometimes referred to as the assumption of referentiality); it is in the writing of the memoirs that Beauvoir actually forges a coherent self-identity (or perhaps, to be more exact, a series of narrative selves each situated in place and time). It is important to bear in mind the split between the past self who is represented and the self who narrates.

The autobiographical pact

In her memoirs, Beauvoir communicates directly with her readers. Like other autobiographers, she negotiates what is referred to as an autobiographical pact with them, making her intentions explicit. However, she does not in fact do this in the first volume of her memoirs. It has been suggested that this is possibly because of uncertainty over its status and anxiety about its reception. As a result of Beauvoir's failure to make her intentions clear, some readers have completely missed her irony and accepted *Memoirs of a Dutiful Daughter* as a straightforward representation of a bourgeois milieu, failing to take into account Beauvoir's attempts to liberate herself from it. In this first volume, it seems that Beauvoir conceives of her readers as benign, generous and understanding. In subsequent volumes, Beauvoir's relationship with her readers changes. She anticipates their criticisms and deals with them head on. In fact, by the end of *Force of Circumstance*, Beauvoir appears to be quite alienated from her readers whom she sees as middle-class.

WOMEN AND AUTOBIOGRAPHY

Until fairly recently, autobiography was seen as a masculine tradition and women's texts were not included in the accepted canon of autobiographical writing. It was not that women were not producing autobiography, but that what they wrote was considered to be unimportant, crude or illegitimate. Writing about themselves was somehow perceived as inappropriate for women. In Beauvoir's case, the writing of a multi-volume autobiography has been seen by some as evidence of narcissism and self-centredness (an accusation unlikely to be leveled at male autobiographers). Beauvoir does not address the question of her marginality in relation to the genre. She took the politically important step of constituting herself as a subject, writing herself into the canon, deliberately associating her memoirs with the memoirs of Pepys and Rousseau, for instance. Her four volumes of memoirs are one of the longest autobiographies ever written by a woman.

The memoirs were not written to form a unified work. Each of the four volumes has its own distinct personality.

MEMOIRS OF A DUTIFUL DAUGHTER

Beauvoir had been thinking about writing about herself for a long time when she actually began the first volume of her memoirs in October 1956. This volume covers her life up to the age of 21, the period 1908–29. It was published in October 1958. It is divided into four parts. The periods covered in the different parts get shorter as Beauvoir gets older, so that later events are dealt with in more detail:

* childhood up until the age of ten when Beauvoir meets Zaza

* school years after the move to the Rue de Rennes due to the change in the Beauvoir family's fortunes

* under-graduate studies

* 1928–29, post-graduate studies, meeting with Sartre and death of Zaza.

Beauvoir describes her repressive upbringing and her growing independence as she escapes from traditional class and gender roles. The year 1929 was a crucial turning point in Beauvoir's life; her formal education ended, she left home, was economically independent and met Sartre. The focus throughout *Memoirs of a Dutiful Daughter* is very much on Beauvoir's thoughts, feelings, attitudes and relationships. She adopts a detached, ironical tone and is often very critical of herself as a child, so the memoir comes across as frank, open and honest. Much of the irony is directed at the bourgeoisie; writing in 1956, Beauvoir wanted all the more to separate herself from this class that she had come to hold responsible for Zaza's death and that she saw as colluding in the atrocities committed in the Algerian War.

THE PRIME OF LIFE

Beauvoir began *The Prime of Life* in the summer of 1958 and submitted the manuscript in May 1960. It was published in November the same year. It covers Beauvoir's life from the summer of 1929, following her success in the *agrégation* and her meeting with Sartre, until the Liberation of Paris in August 1944. It is written in two parts, originally published in two volumes. The first ends just before the outbreak of World War II in 1939, another key moment in Beauvoir's life. *The Prime of Life* was conceived as a sequel to *Memoirs of a Dutiful Daughter*; Beauvoir wished to explore in it what use she had made of the freedom she had won in 1929.

It is a very different book from the first volume of the memoirs. It is longer, more colloquial, less carefully constructed. Despite this, or perhaps even because of it, *The Prime of Life* communicates Beauvoir's energy and appetite for life. The focus naturally moves away from her family to her circle of friends and acquaintances. Sartre is a central figure and much of the book is taken up with the views that Beauvoir shares with him. Some of the important themes in *The Prime of Life* are:

* Beauvoir's relationship with Sartre, their disagreements and her fears of becoming over-dependent on him

* her relationship with Olga and the failure of the 'trio'

* her first serious illness

* her early writing career and the effect the success of *She Came to Stay* had on her reputation

* the evolution of her philosophical ideas

* her growing awareness of the importance of politics

* travel – Beauvoir made 56 trips during this period

* her experiences during the Occupation.

The book is divided into chapters that cover periods of various lengths – school years, holidays, weekends – as the narrative demands. To relate the first ten months of the war, Beauvoir inserts edited versions of her diaries in the text. The diary form gives readers a vivid, detailed impression of what her daily life was like. Also new in *The Prime of Life* are the overviews where Beauvoir sums up the significance of the events in her life. Her willingness to look critically at herself gives readers a sense that she is being open and honest.

FORCE OF CIRCUMSTANCE

Beauvoir began the third volume of her memoirs in 1961 and finished it in spring 1963. It covers the period from the Liberation in August 1944 to the autumn of 1962, following the end of the Algerian War. It was published in October 1963. Significantly, the gap between the time represented and the time of writing is very much narrower. As Beauvoir is much closer to the events she describes, she is more emotionally involved and her tone is less detached.

Beauvoir hesitated before writing *Force of Circumstance* but, in the end, she decided to go ahead with the third volume of her memoirs to bear witness to recent events in France. In this sense, *Force of Circumstance* is a much less personal work. Self-critical analysis is still in evidence and Beauvoir's emotional responses and attitudes are vividly portrayed, but she was clearly writing to make a political point: she wanted her readers to feel bad about the Algerian War. The book as a whole is much more overtly political than any of the other three volumes. The existentialist title draws readers' attention to the weight of situation in human existence.

Force of Circumstance is divided into two parts. The disintegration of the Left after the Liberation provides the context for part one; the war in Algeria forms the context in part two. Some key themes are:

* Existentialism and the impact of fame and popularity on writers and intellectuals

* Beauvoir's writing – the genesis, writing, publication, reception and commentary of the books written during this extremely productive time for her

* politics – particularly Sartre's political positions

* the Algerian war and the French government's policies

* travel – accounts of the 87 trips Beauvoir made during this period take up roughly a quarter of the text

Force of Circumstance is somewhat uneven in terms of the space Beauvoir devotes to different aspects of her experience; 'too bad' she said! The overviews which are a feature of *The Prime of Life* are present here too. Also as in the previous volume, a number of edited diary extracts are inserted in the text.

Force of Circumstance as a whole is clearly inflected by Beauvoir's mood at the time she was writing it; her growing awareness of ageing and death combined with the impact of the Algerian War left her depressed, disillusioned and alienated in the early 1960s. The final, ambiguous comment she makes in *Force of Circumstance* has given rise to a great deal of controversy: 'The promises have all been kept. And yet, turning an incredulous gaze towards that young and credulous girl, I realize with stupor how much I was gypped' (*Force of Circumstance*, p. 674).

The final word of the comment – *flouée* in French – has been variously translated: 'gypped', 'cheated', 'swindled'. Some – particularly those who disapprove of the life choices she made – have relished the idea that it is a general admission of failure on Beauvoir's part. More convincing is Beauvoir's explanation that her bitter disappointment is the result of the gap between the promise the world had held for the naive, privileged young girl that she had been, and the reality of horror, torture and misery in the world.

ALL SAID AND DONE

The final volume of Beauvoir's memoirs, *All Said and Done*, covers a ten-year period from autumn 1962. It was published in the autumn of 1972. The title is somewhat curious. Beauvoir appears to want to sum up a life that was far from over – she would live a further 14 years or so. In *The Prime of Life* she says that starting to write about herself had been a rash undertaking – once you begin, it is impossible to break off; in *All Said and Done* it is almost as if she is impatient to have done with her memoirs.

This volume stands out from the others mainly because it is structured very differently. Whereas the narrative in the first three volumes was chronological, *All Said and Done* is organized around themes. The chronological narrative of the earlier volumes had been partly philosophically motivated; it conveyed the purpose and progression of a life whose meaning was deferred. In contrast, Beauvoir was writing *All Said and Done* with most of her life behind her and it seemed apt to go some way towards summing up her life which, she said, had changed very little between 1962 and 1971. Various aspects of her life are picked up again and analysed anew. In some ways, the volume appears to be an attempt to correct certain misconceptions.

In particular, Beauvoir set out to convince her readers that they had misunderstood the final sentence in *Force of Circumstance*. The gloom of that volume has disappeared and her tone in *All Said and Done* is deliberately up-beat; her aim is to present her life as an unmitigated success. Sadly, Beauvoir in this final volume of her memoirs, seems to feel she must deny that sadness, loneliness and pain are part of her existence.

The book is divided into eight chapters, which deal with the following themes:

* Aspects of Beauvoir's life as a whole: freedom and choice versus chance; continuities; her daily life at that time, including the process of ageing; friends and acquaintances; dreams.

* Beauvoir's writing.

* The arts: reading; films; plays; the nature of culture; education.

* Travel – three chapters are devoted to her travels; one mainly to her trips in France and Italy, another to her stay in Japan and the third to her trips to Russia.

* International politics.

* French politics including the events of May 1968 and feminism.

Beauvoir's commitment to fighting oppression emerges clearly from the pages of *All Said and Done*. Overall, the tone is less personal and more informative. Personal analysis and self-criticism have given way to description and a chronicle of events.

LETTERS AND WAR DIARIES

Beauvoir kept a diary intermittently throughout her life. It is important to remember that she did not write her letters and diaries for publication. During her lifetime, apart from the edited versions of the diaries and a few letters included in the memoirs, she refused to make them public and, indeed, for many years she told anyone who asked that her letters to Sartre had been lost. These personal writings are not carefully constructed, well thought-through commentaries on culture, politics or philosophy. The letters she wrote when she was separated from Sartre partly served the purpose of satisfying his appetite for gossip. Additionally, it appears that Beauvoir frequently turned to her personal writing to cope with anxiety, fear, loneliness and misery. This is supported by an examination of the diary extracts included in the memoirs.

Beauvoir gives two reasons for including them:

* when the diaries are lively or amusing

* when she feels it is best not to try to recreate how she felt but to give the exact words she wrote at the time.

The extracts actually reveal her emotional anguish.

TRUTH

When Beauvoir's letters to Sartre and a number of the diaries she wrote at the beginning of World War II were published posthumously in 1990, discrepancies between them and the memoirs focused attention on the question of Beauvoir's truthfulness. She stands accused of mythologizing, of deliberately distorting the facts of her experience to create a rosy picture.

Beauvoir repeatedly emphasizes the fact that her memoirs are truthful. In the autobiographical pact that she makes with her readers at the beginning of *The Prime of Life*, she undertakes not to lie to us. However, she does not promise to tell us everything. Nor, she tells us, can she guarantee that she will not make mistakes.

There can never be an exact match between lived experience and the representation of that experience. An autobiographer necessarily reworks lived experience. As Beauvoir herself points out, selectivity is inevitable. She naturally selects from her experience in line with her overall intention, which is to represent herself as an intellectual and a writer. Her memoirs are not intended to be a 'confession', which would give prominence to her personal life. Beauvoir's diaries give a much more complex picture of her personal relationships than her memoirs. For example, in *Memoirs of a Dutiful Daughter*, Sartre is constructed straightforwardly as her ideal partner, whereas the diaries of the time show that Beauvoir's life-long commitment to him was not so self-evident.

There are bound to be omissions. There is a sense in which what is omitted – that is Beauvoir's silences – also tells us about Beauvoir and her era by showing us what she would not or could not speak about. It is the case that Beauvoir writes allusively about her relationships with women in her diaries but does not mention them at all in her memoirs. This is understandable given the social strictures against homosexuality that prevailed at the time. However, not all the omissions can be explained by social pressures. For instance, Beauvoir's memoirs do not mention Arlette, Sartre's companion and adoptive daughter with whom Beauvoir's relations were difficult. It is hard not to see this omission and other similar omissions or evasions as a distortion of the truth. Sometimes Beauvoir does indicate gaps and also points out where she has been mistaken or misled readers. For example, in *Force of Circumstance*, she admits that *The Prime of Life* did not give an accurate picture of her relationship with Sartre (p. 134).

Beauvoir makes the point that she wishes to protect certain people by not including their stories in her memoirs. Others, she protects by using pseudonyms. (This, combined with her habit of giving her friends and acquaintances nicknames which are used in the letters and the fact that sometimes different names are used in the English translation of the letters, can be confusing for readers.) Despite Beauvoir's claims, it is nevertheless the case that she does not always protect all her friends, and in fact is capable of writing quite damning accounts of them. For instance, she ignored Bianca Lamblin's specific request not to be included in the memoirs; the portrayal of Nathalie Sorokine is extremely harsh; Algren never forgave Beauvoir for writing what she did about their relationship in *The Prime of Life*.

Particular relationships, incidents and experiences are sometimes reworked and represented a number of times in Beauvoir's fiction, letters, diaries and memoirs. For example, Beauvoir's seduction of Bost is recounted in *She Came to Stay* and the letters but is omitted from the memoirs. A comparative analysis of such incidents is interesting because it reveals the nature and extent of Beauvoir's selectivity and omissions. As regards the differences between the diaries and the memoirs, it is worth remembering that, unlike the memoirs, Beauvoir's diaries show how her perspective evolves with the passage of time and besides, it is only reasonable to expect that when she comes to write her memoirs some twenty years later, her perspective will have changed again. That being said, what is problematical is that when Beauvoir uses extracts from her diaries in the memoirs, she fails to acknowledge that these have been adapted.

Although some have attempted it, establishing a hierarchy of truth based on the comparison of the different accounts in the various genres is a somewhat pointless exercise. (The suggestion is that the diaries are truer than the memoirs which are truer than the fiction, for example.) Ultimately, there is no basis for assuming that any version is any truer in an absolute sense than any other. After all, the diaries were not intended for publication and so factual accuracy was unlikely to be paramount in Beauvoir's mind when she was writing them. The emotional intensity of the fiction may well seem at times to be more 'true' than the accounts related in the memoirs.

* * *SUMMARY* * *

- The four volumes of Beauvoir's memoirs make up one of the longest autobiographies ever written by a woman.

- Beauvoir believed in the universal dimension of her memoirs; the portrait of her life sheds light on the lives of others.

- Testimony: Beauvoir wrote her memoirs to bear witness to her time and to bring about change.

- Beauvoir also wrote her memoirs to preserve her past selves and to construct a coherent self-identity.

- Discrepancies between Beauvoir's letters and war diaries and the memoirs have raised questions about her truthfulness. It is impossible to establish a hierarchy of truth, but a comparative analysis can reveal the nature of the selectivity and the reworking of experience that operate in the memoirs.

7 A Twentieth-Century Intellectual

In the French context, the term 'intellectual' has a special significance which is difficult to transpose into British and American contexts. For many years, intellectuals in France have had celebrity status. The French public looks to intellectuals for an understanding of the issues of the day. With very few exceptions, serious writers, philosophers and academics are just not well-known public figures in the same way in Britain and North America.

Beauvoir was a true intellectual in that she believed utterly in the importance of words. As an intellectual committed to the socialist ideal of a just, classless society, she used words as her weapon to expose inequality, oppression, exploitation and injustice. For her, writing was action. In the post-war decades, the journal *Les Temps modernes*, set up by Beauvoir and Sartre, was an influential forum for left-wing debate. These debates were literary and philosophical as well as political. Beauvoir wrote articles, gave interviews, held press conferences, signed manifestos, spoke at meetings, and went on demonstrations, some of which were illegal. As she became more prominent, Beauvoir was not afraid to use her high profile to challenge the establishment and act as a shield for others whose lack of public fame made them vulnerable to retaliation by the authorities.

At this point, however, it is necessary to mention briefly the particular place of women intellectuals in France. It is sadly true that they tend to be marginalized and that their work is often greeted with hostility. Beauvoir has been frequently portrayed as a bluestocking and criticized for being a cold, unfeminine woman. There is also a marked tendency to judge women intellectuals' work in relation to the male intellectuals around them, though the reverse is rarely, if ever, true. In Beauvoir's case, her ideas have not only been attributed to Sartre, but to Algren and Lanzmann as well.

POLITICS

Until the outbreak of World War II in 1939, Beauvoir did not interest herself in politics, preferring instead to focus on freedom and abstract philosophical questions. The war was a turning point in her life; she discovered solidarity and the pressure of political reality: 'History took hold of me, and never let go thereafter', she says (*The Prime of Life*, p. 359). Looking back, she felt shame at her selfish individualism in the 1930s.

Generally speaking, Beauvoir thought that, in politics, even when they support the government, intellectuals should always remain a potential source of criticism and opposition to policies and should never agree to be part of a government. Sartre was always far more interested in day-to-day politics than Beauvoir, and to some extent, her main concern was to support him. However, she was very much in sympathy with politics to do with developing countries and oppressed peoples everywhere.

THE POST-WAR PERIOD

Beauvoir and Sartre's anti-Gaullist stance never wavered. General Charles de Gaulle, who headed the first post-war government in France, stood for everything they despised; he was right-wing, conservative, bourgeois and catholic. By the 1950s, Beauvoir had come to see him as a dangerous paranoid despot, on a par with Stalin.

As for the Left, Beauvoir and Sartre were concerned when the unity that had characterized the Resistance began to disintegrate. Beauvoir was not prepared to join the Communists because, although she accepted the importance of the class struggle, she objected to the authoritarianism and disregard for human rights of Stalinism. With the beginning of the Cold War in 1947, Beauvoir and Sartre had greater sympathy for the Soviet Union than for the States, but found the choice between the two powers an impossible one to make. They looked for a middle way and, in 1948, supported a new political grouping – the *Rassemblement Démocratique Révolutionnaire* (RDR) – which was intended to unite all non-Communist socialist groups in an attempt to create a Europe independent of both the US and USSR. When this ended in failure in 1949, the couple withdrew from politics for a time.

In 1952, Sartre started working with the French Communist Party, not because his views had altered, nor because the Communist Party was any different, but because he was finding it harder and harder to tolerate the hypocrisy of the bourgeoisie and wanted to end his political isolation. Beauvoir was initially reluctant to follow Sartre's lead, but, as Beauvoir puts it, Lanzmann doggedly challenged her convictions and gradually convinced her to adopt Sartre's point of view. Beauvoir was never a Marxist in the strict sense of the term, but Marxism did influence her views on exploitation and alienation. Beauvoir and Sartre broke with the Communists in 1956 over the Soviet invasion of Hungary and accepted their political isolation.

ANTI-IMPERIALISM

Beauvoir found herself in opposition to the majority of French people for the first time over the colonial wars in Indo-China. She was delighted at the defeat of France in Vietnam in 1954, but shocked and distressed to find herself so at odds with her fellow citizens.

From 1954, the Algerian War of Independence caused deep divisions in French society. There was little public opposition to the war in the early 1950s and Beauvoir's stand for Algerian independence made her very unpopular among a large section of the French public. She campaigned against French atrocities in Algeria, publishing accounts of massacres, rapes and torture in *Les Temps modernes*. When de Gaulle was recalled to power to deal with the crisis in 1958, Beauvoir campaigned against the new constitution he proposed and was devastated by the huge majority in favour of the Fifth Republic in the referendum.

The summer of 1960 saw repressive measures introduced by the government. As a signatory of the 'Manifesto of the 121' against French policy in Algeria, Beauvoir was banned from appearing on radio or television. She and Sartre tried to have themselves charged for signing the Manifesto, but the authorities were reluctant to take legal action against such a high-profile couple. Beauvoir saw France becoming more and more like a police state. Public opinion was shifting in favour of Algerian independence (influenced in part by the Manifesto), but these were violent times. Beauvoir and Sartre even had to go into hiding for a time because of threats from the terrorist *Organisation de l'Armée Secrète, OAS* (Secret Army Organization). Bombings were not uncommon and both Beauvoir and Sartre were targets a number of times; on 7 January 1962, the building where they thought they were safe was bombed, and Sartre's flat was seriously damaged by an explosion a few days later.

Beauvoir was outraged by the case of a young Algerian woman, Djamila Boupacha, accused of spying, who had been raped and tortured by French soldiers. She agreed to campaign on her behalf. Thanks to the international attention that Beauvoir's interest attracted, the case was transferred from Algiers to France. She wrote the preface to the book about the case, written by the activist lawyer, Gisèle Halimi in an attempt to stop the torture and mutilation of Algerian women. Beauvoir's fierce attack on what she called the genocide taking place in Algeria and her outspoken support for Algerian nationalism provoked more anger. Beauvoir's name appeared as co-author so she could share responsibility and any punishment meted out by the French authorities. For Beauvoir, peace in Algeria in 1962 'came too late to console [her] for the price it had cost' (*Force of Circumstance*, p. 658). As a result of their stance on Algerian independence, Beauvoir and Sartre would be seen by many as a symbol of defiance to the establishment.

MAY 1968
In the late 1960s, unrest among students in the United States and throughout Europe was growing. The student-led uprising, in Paris in May 1968, ended Beauvoir's and Sartre's political isolation. Students were protesting against rigid hierarchies and the power the technocrats held in

France at that time. Beauvoir hoped that the student revolt would lead to the overthrow of the Gaullist régime. She and Sartre signed a manifesto supporting the students and calling for workers and intellectuals to follow suit. In particular, Beauvoir's sympathies lay with the Maoists, whom she saw as revolutionary socialists. Unlike the traditional left wing, they were not prepared to accept the system but sought to overthrow it. However, hopes that the régime would be overturned were dashed when the authorities restored order. Nevertheless, 1968 marked a radicalization of the couple's political views and, from this point on, Beauvoir was more committed than ever to espousing radical causes in favour of the working classes and the oppressed.

RADICAL CAUSES

Beauvoir was an outspoken critic of the American war in Vietnam. She was extremely angry at the unjustness of the American position. In 1966, Beauvoir and Sartre took part in the Bertrand Russell International War Crimes Tribunal, set up to protest against the US presence in Vietnam and to bring American action there to trial. The aim was to stir up public opinion against the war all over the world, particularly in the US.

Beauvoir's involvement with the women's movement dates from around 1970, although for more than a decade she had been gradually devoting more and more of her energy to the cause of women. (Her feminist activism will be considered in the following chapter.)

Beauvoir, like Sartre, was an advocate of a free press. In the early 1970s, Beauvoir supported two revolutionary newspapers, banned by the government, *La Cause du Peuple* and *L'Idiot international*, for a time taking on the editorship of the latter. Demonstrations were held, meetings organized, copies of the illegal publications distributed in the street and interviews given to the French and foreign media. Beauvoir defied the authorities to arrest and prosecute her but they never did.

Beauvoir campaigned tirelessly on behalf of the oppressed. She signed 72 of the 488 manifestos published in *Le Monde* between 1958 and

1969, making her the third-most frequent signatory overall and the most frequent woman signatory. When a journalist asked Beauvoir if signing so many appeals did any good, she replied that possibly a few lives had been saved but that in any event, it was impossible not to sign. If only a few out of the many appeals were successful then it meant you had to try.

TRAVELS

After the war, and as their fame grew, Beauvoir's and Sartre's political commitments and the causes they supported took them abroad. When the couple were the official guests of governments or organizations, it is clear that Beauvoir was initially invited as Sartre's companion. However, increasingly, as her own reputation grew, alongside the official engagements, Beauvoir was sought out by the less powerful, particularly women, who wanted to hear what Beauvoir had to say about their situation. Beauvoir was also invited to visit different countries and address certain organizations in her own right.

Beauvoir's travels took her all over the world.

In fact, Beauvoir did not enjoy public speaking. She was shy and awkward when she had to stand up and speak before an audience, afraid she would disappoint her listeners or fail to achieve what she intended. She knew she spoke too fast but could not help herself. She nevertheless felt she must make herself give lectures, because of her power to influence the way people thought.

Many have commented on the fact that Beauvoir's memoirs, particularly in the 1960s and 1970s, very much resemble a travelogue. The following highlights some of the more important and influential trips she made.

Post-Liberation years

In 1945, Beauvoir travelled to Portugal via Spain as the official correspondent of the newspaper *Combat* and to give lectures on the situation in France during the Occupation. On her return, she wrote a series of newspaper articles condemning General Franco and the Portuguese dictator, Antonio Salazar. Lecture tours in Tunisia, Algeria and Italy followed. Beauvoir, sponsored by the *Alliance Française*, spoke about French literature and explained and defended existentialism. Finally, in 1947, Beauvoir got her long-held wish to go to the United States. Her lecture tour lasted four months. She was billed as 'France's No. 2 Existentialist' and gave talks on the moral responsibility of post-war writers and discussed art and politics on university campuses all over America. Her ambivalent impressions of the country are recounted in *America Day by Day*, published in 1948. As a record of her fascination and disappointments, Beauvoir's book brings the country to life for her readers. As might be expected, she is critical of the right-wing politics and anti-Communism she found there.

The 1950s

In 1950, Beauvoir travelled to Africa with Sartre. They visited Algeria, Mali, Upper Volta, Ivory Coast and Morocco. They had wanted to contact the *Rassemblement Démocratique Africain* (*RDA*), who were resisting the authorities, to find out what was really happening in Africa so they could publish their findings in *Les Temps modernes*. In fact, because of the couple's isolation from the Communist Party, they never met the *RDA* and, although they were well received by the authorities, what was the couple's first political trip as such was a severe disappointment.

In 1955, Beauvoir travelled to China with Sartre. For two months, they were official guests of the Communist government who wanted them to witness the country's progress. Her impressions of China were published in *The Long March* in 1957. Beauvoir wanted to defend China and act as the country's advocate in the West and her account is very favourable. She believed she was witnessing the construction of socialism. In fact, she and Sartre saw only what the government officials wanted them to. Critics did not like the book and Beauvoir came to agree with them; in later years she would describe it as 'hasty journalism', 'of no value', 'a dishonest undertaking' (Deirdre Bair, *Simone de Beauvoir*, p. 456). However, the trip to China was important in that it transformed Beauvoir's view of the world – the sheer size of the Chinese population and the poverty she encountered there forced her to reassess her own civilization.

Beauvoir and Sartre visited Moscow briefly on their way to China and then again, for one week, on their way home. These visits would be the first of many. Beauvoir was struck by the relative wealth of the Soviet Union after the poverty of China. A great deal of construction was going on there in 1955. She and Sartre met a lot of Soviet writers and critics while they were there. Her memoirs describe the sumptuous banquet they attended, where the food was washed down with glass after glass of wine and vodka. Beauvoir herself wrote two articles, gave interviews and spoke on the radio. She was so exhausted, she spent her last day in Moscow in bed.

The 1960s

Beauvoir and Sartre travelled widely throughout the 1960s. In Cuba (1960), the couple were able to witness the early stages of a socialist revolution. They were photographed with Fidel Castro and Che Guevara and escorted on a tour of Cuba by Castro himself. The new Cuban regime wanted Beauvoir and Sartre to tell the world about the revolution. Beauvoir was enthusiastic, though in later years, she would criticize the Cuban revolution for failing to live up to its promises.

In 1960, a group of Brazilian writers and intellectuals invited Beauvoir and Sartre to visit their country to talk about the Cuban revolution and to see what life was like in an underdeveloped country. The couple covered 7500 miles during their two-month-long visit, and were given a very warm welcome wherever they went to give lectures and interviews. They were made honorary citizens by the city of Rio.

In 1961, Beauvoir went alone to Belgium to give a series of lectures. She spoke to a group of extreme left-wing students about the Algerian question, under the title 'The Intellectual and the Government'. While she was there, she also met trade unionists to discuss the general strike that was intended to reorganize the country's economy on a socialist basis. In September 1966, Beauvoir and Sartre were welcomed like stars in Japan – crowds of young people and hundreds of photographers and reporters were at Tokyo airport to greet them. Beauvoir gave a series of lectures on writing to large audiences. During the month-long stay, Beauvoir interviewed women dock workers in Kyoto for Japanese television and also, in Hiroshima, under a media glare, met victims of the atomic bomb.

Beauvoir denounced the Russian invasion of Czechoslovakia in August 1968 and visited the country the following November. The tragedy of Prague affected her deeply, and in 1971 she wrote that the Russians had disappointed all her hopes (*All Said and Done*, p. 336). The year 1968 marked the end of Beauvoir's and Sartre's overtly political travelling.

---

* * *SUMMARY* * *

- As an intellectual, Beauvoir used words to fight inequality, oppression, exploitation and injustice.

- Beauvoir wrote articles, gave interviews, held press conferences, signed manifestos, spoke at meetings, and went on demonstrations, some of which were banned.

- She used her celebrity status to defy the authorities and to protect others from possible retaliation.

- She travelled widely.

The Feminist Movement

Feminism is undoubtedly one of the most influential and revolutionary movements of the twentieth century. Simone de Beauvoir's relationship with the women's movement is characterized by change over time, and her contribution to it is, at times, fiercely contested. There is no simple answer to the question of her contribution to second-wave feminism, that is feminism since 1970. Beauvoir's connections with the women's movement are complex.

BEAUVOIR'S CHANGE OF HEART

When she wrote *The Second Sex*, the work to which she owes much of her reputation as a feminist, Beauvoir did not consider herself to be a feminist at all. Nor did she see her book as feminist, but as a theoretical study or philosophical essay. When she wrote *The Second Sex*, Beauvoir believed that the overthrow of capitalism would bring about the liberation of women and make them men's equals. Her aim in writing her study of women was to help her contemporaries to understand themselves and their situation.

In 1966, Beauvoir said that interpretations of her feminism as not radically feminist were false, but it was not until the early 1970s that Simone de Beauvoir publicly defined herself as a feminist. In an interview with Alice Schwarzer in 1972, she explains what led her to become a feminist activist. Before 1970, according to Beauvoir, feminism was reformist and legalist, whereas the new feminism is radical. Beauvoir rejects reformist positions; for her, it is not a question of women finding their place in society as it is, but of transforming society itself. She is not only demanding an improvement in women's condition but also the destruction of the very system that engenders inequalities and injustice. By the 1970s, she had come to realize that socialism would not lead to the emancipation of women and that women must work for their emancipation themselves, independently of the class struggle.

A DRIVING FORCE OF FEMINISM

The Second Sex, published in 1949, preceded by twenty years the rise of feminism in the late 1960s and 1970s, yet this book exerted a profound influence on the second-wave feminist movement in France and, particularly, in the USA and the UK. There is widespread agreement on the central importance of Beauvoir's book. It certainly influenced a generation of women who read it for its analyses of women's oppression and male domination. Many feminists have expressed their feelings of gratitude and admiration towards Beauvoir, who helped them to understand women's condition.

Beauvoir, along with many others, considered her book to be useful in that it provided the women's movement with a theoretical tool. Yvette Roudy, French Minister for Women's Rights in 1981, thought that without the theoretical framework of *The Second Sex*, the feminist stuggles of the 1970s would not have been so successful.

Feminists in the 1970s picked up again many of the ideas developed by Simone de Beauvoir in *The Second Sex*, including:

* the denunciation of cultural myths

* the questioning of marriage, the family and motherhood

* the boredom of housewives

* the economic dependency of married women

* the taboos surrounding women's sex lives and their lack of freedom.

However, it was not so much that the new generation of feminists consciously turned to Beauvoir's book for inspiration, as that many of its ideas, that had seemed so revolutionary or controversial in 1949, were, in the 1970s, commonplace in feminist circles and were even becoming so in society at large. *The Second Sex* was part of the outlook on the world that feminist activists in the 1970s shared.

'FRENCH FEMINISM'

In the French context, the terms 'feminist' and 'emancipation of women' do not always sit comfortably together. An important strand of the women's movement in France is explicitly anti-feminist, by which is meant anti-egalitarian. Paradoxically, this anti-feminist strand of the movement, *Psychanalyse et politique* (Psychoanalysis and politics), registered the name and logo *Mouvement de Libération des Femmes – MLF* (Womens Liberation Movement) as trademarks and so became *the* official women's movement in France. To make things even more complicated, this is the strand of the movement that is referred to as 'French feminism' in Anglo-American writings on feminist theory.

This self-declared anti-feminist strand of the women's movement rejects Simone de Beauvoir and her work, ironically, accusing her of reformism and even of misogyny because of what they see as her devalorization of feminine difference. Their theoretical positions are diametrically opposed. For Beauvoir, accepting the existence of specifically feminine qualities would mean acknowledging the existence of a specifically female nature, the myth invented to justify the oppression of women. For differentialist feminists, it is this feminine difference that has been repressed under patriarchy which will be the source of women's liberation. They accuse women seeking the social equality of the sexes (including Beauvoir) of wanting to eradicte sexual difference.

1980s: BEAUVOIR RE-EVALUATED

By the 1980s, Beauvoir's feminist credentials were also being put in question by a number of feminist writers who did not belong to the differentialist strand of feminism. Hostile criticism of *The Second Sex* was widespread. For many feminists, *The Second Sex* was in many ways an embarassment. Beauvoir's text was criticized for a number of reasons:

* The anti-feminism of existentialism: the duality between transcendence and immanence implicitly evokes the masculine/feminine opposition. Also, despite her attempts to not accuse women of a lack of authenticity and of bad faith, Beauvoir nevertheless ends up blaming women for their situation.

* Disgust for the female body: for example, in passages describing female sexual initiation, women are compared to inert, empty receptacles and their sexual arousal to the oozing of a decomposing corpse.

* Masculine bias: the glamorization of maleness and the adoption of masculine values. Motherhood is confined to the category of immanence.

* False universalism: Beauvoir writes as if all women are the same.

These criticisms have, in turn, been subject to analysis. While accepting that there are real difficulties for feminist readers of *The Second Sex* today, some critics have shown that such criticisms can sometimes be based on misundertandings and misreadings of the text.

The rejection of Beauvoir by feminist intellectuals in the 1980s has been seen by a number of commentators as analogous to the rejection of a mother by her daughters. Of course, to acknowledge these motivations is not to dismiss the criticisms levelled at *The Second Sex*, nor to excuse or explain away the obvious difficulties that it poses. Ultimately, however, we should resist the dual temptation to either reduce Beauvoir's text to nothing but a misogynistic, anti-feminist attack on women or to elevate it to a flawless accomplishment.

Today, there is evidence of renewed interest in *The Second Sex*. A number of feminist theorists are looking to Beauvoir for a way of reconciling the possibility of political action with the notion of identity as freely constructed. In fact, *The Second Sex* provides us with a definition of gender and identity that is neither essentialist – based on notions of feminine nature – nor post-feminist – based on the dissolution of the subject. Beauvoir's account of women's condition shows that it is possible to struggle for change even under oppression.

BEAUVOIR'S FEMINIST ACTIVISM

So far, we have considered Beauvoir's contribution to the feminist movement in terms of her theoretical contribution. She also made a major contribution in terms of activism. In the 1970s, she began to take part in collective action and campaigned alongside other, younger women, to improve women's lives. As she said to Alice Schwarzer in an

Beauvoir took part in feminist demonstrations in the seventies.

interview which first appeared in *Marie-Claire* in 1976, 'I am not a militant in the strict sense of the word – after all, I'm not thirty anymore, I'm a sixty-seven year old intellectual whose weapons are her words – but I follow the women's movement at very close hand, and I am at its disposal' (*Simone de Beauvoir Today*, p. 69). Her words are an accurate reflection of her relationship with the younger feminists; despite the age difference and her celebrity status, she did not seek to impose her authority but encouraged and supported the younger women. Typically, her aim was to play a prominent role in protests in order to shield other women from possible reprisals from the authorities.

In particular, in the early days of the women's movement, Beauvoir campaigned with materialist feminists for the legalization of abortion and free contraception. She signed the *Manifeste des 343* (Manifesto of the 343), declaring publicly with many ordinary woman as well as other well-known women, that she had had an illegal abortion. Theoretically, by signing the manifesto, she risked arrest and imprisonment but, in fact, her fame made her virtually untouchable. Beauvoir had never actually had an abortion although she had paid for abortions for other women and sometimes allowed them to be performed in her flat. Beauvoir played a major role in the meetings at the *Mutualité* meeting hall in Paris, where, in May 1972, five thousand women gathered to denounce the crimes perpetrated against women, ranging from rape and violence to everyday discrimination. She became president of *Choisir*, the pro-choice organization, for a time, and also president of the *Ligue du droit des femmes* (League for the Rights of Women) which combats discrimination against women, especially in the workplace. She also contributed her time and money to help women survivors of domestic violence and rape. In 1972, Beauvoir appeared as witness in the Bobigny abortion trial in which a young woman of 17 and her mother were being prosecuted. She began a regular column in *Les Temps modernes*, called 'Everyday Sexism', which atttacked examples of sexist language and sexist images of women used by the press, politicians and advertisers. With other Marxist feminists in 1977, Beauvoir launched the journal, *Questions féministes*, agreeing to take full editorial responsibility should the journal fall foul of the authorities.

In 1982, Beauvoir became Honorary Chair of the *Commission Femmes et Culture* (Commission for Women and Culture), set up by Yvette Roudy, socialist Minister for Women's Rights. The Commission, which came to be called informally the *Commission Beauvoir*, was charged with producing concrete proposals for change. Far from remaining in her honorary role, Beauvoir was an active participant in the Commission's work.

Throughout the 1970s, Beauvoir's position evolved, becoming more radical. The process of radicalization can be traced in her writings and in the interviews she gave during the 1970s and 1980s. Beauvoir's tone gets harder, more bitter, and even more aggressive after 1970. Less emphasis is placed on theoretical and philosophical considerations, and more is placed on concrete ideas and practical solutions to the problems women face.

Beauvoir approved of the new generation of feminists for rejecting her optimistic vision of the future at the end of *The Second Sex* and admired their determination to take their fate into their own hands. They were right to fight!

In January 1999, hundreds of women, of all ages, from all over the world, gathered in Paris to celebrate the 50th anniversary of the publication of *The Second Sex*. The conference was an opportunity to remember Simone de Beauvoir's contribution to feminism both in terms of theory and activism. Numerous testimonies revealed that Beauvoir has been an inspiration to many women. Her place in the women's movement may be contested and often marked by ambivalence, but it is a place which is nevertheless of crucial importance.

* * * SUMMARY * * *

- Beauvoir publicly defined herself as a feminist in the early 1970s. She espoused radical feminism which sought to transform society.

- She owes much of her reputation as a feminist to *The Second Sex*, which provided the women's movement with a theoretical tool.

- Beauvoir is rejected by the anti-feminist, anti-egalitarian strand of the women's movement in France because, in their view, she devalorizes feminine difference.

- Hostile criticism of *The Second Sex* in the 1980s has given way to renewed interest in Beauvoir's ideas today; she offers women a theory of identity that allows for political action.

- Feminist activism: Beauvoir participated in collective action to bring about change and improve the lives of women.

9 Beauvoir Today

How is Simone de Beauvoir remembered today? Some remember her as Sartre's companion. She herself could see no contradiction between what she wrote in *The Second Sex* and the way she recognized Sartre's genius and dedicated her life to supporting him. In recent years, the traditional view of Beauvoir as Sartre's disciple has been challenged and it is increasingly recognized that she was far more original and had a greater influence on Sartre than she was prepared to admit.

Others remember Beauvoir as a writer. All her life, she remained faithful to her fundamental project of knowing and writing – discovering the world and communicating her understanding to her readers. Beauvoir's writings include philosophy, fiction, drama, autobiography and travel writing and her books have reached a mass readership. In *Force of Circumstance*, 1963, Beauvoir tells us that if, when she was thirty, someone had told her that she would be concerning herself with women's problems and that her most serious public would be made up of women, she would have been surprised and even irritated. But, she has no regrets that it has been so. Through women, Beauvoir says, she has avoided drifting in the universal and taken a limited but real hold upon the world (p. 203).

Beauvoir was aware of the irony that she may be remembered as a feminist, even though she did not think of herself as a feminist until she was in her sixties. *The Second Sex* provided a theoretical framework for second-wave feminism in the 1970s, and Beauvoir was a major figure in the struggle against women's oppression. Today feminist theorists are showing renewed interest in her ideas on the social construction of gender and identity as they do not preclude political praxis.

Beauvoir said, 'I am an intellectual, I take words and truth to be of value' (*Force of Circumstance*, p. 378). All through her life, she used the power of words to bring about change. She was determined to be taken seriously and her example has made it easier for women today to take themselves seriously as intellectuals.

Beauvoir's life is exemplary and, at the same time, individual, with its share of contradictions, conflicts, joy and pain. Beauvoir has had a profound influence on the lives of her readers. She has accomplished what she saw as the role of literature – she has made us feel less alone in the things that separate us absolutely. As a teenager, Beauvoir dreamt of becoming a famous author, loved by her readers. Almost at the end of her writing career in 1972, she was satisfied with her achievement:

> I wanted to make myself exist for others by conveying, as directly as I could, the taste of my own life: I have more or less succeeded. I have some thorough-going enemies, but I have also made many friends among my readers. I asked no more.
>
> (*All Said and Done*, p. 463)

CHRONOLOGY
THE LIFE AND WORK OF SIMONE DE BEAUVOIR

9 January 1908	Born in Paris.
1910	Birth of Hélène (Poupette), her sister.
1913	Starts school – *cours Désir*.
1918	Begins friendship with Zaza.
1919	Family leaves Boulevard Montparnasse and moves to Rue de Rennes.
1922	Loss of faith in God.
1925–28	Undergraduate studies in philosophy
1928–29	Postgraduate studies. Meets Jean-Paul Sartre. Passes the *agrégation* examination. Zaza dies.
1929–31	Writing and private teaching.
1931	Teaching in Marseilles. (Sartre teaching in Le Havre.) Makes first trip abroad (Spain).
1932	Teaching in Rouen.
1933	Begins friendship with Olga Kosakievicz.
1934	'Trio' with Sartre and Olga.
1935	Begins writing *When Things of the Spirit Come First*.
1936	Meets Jacques Bost. Takes up teaching post in Paris. 'Trio' over.
1937	Hospitalized with pulmonary congestion. *When Things of the Spirit Come First* rejected by Gallimard and Grasset publishing houses. Begins writing *She Came to Stay*.
1938	Begins affair with Bost.
1939	World War II begins. (Sartre called up.)
1940	German Occupation. (Sartre in prison camp.)
1941	Father, Georges de Beauvoir dies. *She Came to Stay* accepted for publication. Begins writing *The Blood of Others*. (Sartre released and returns to Paris.)

1943	*She Came to Stay* published. *The Blood of Others* completed. Writes *Pyrrhus et Cinéas*. Begins writing *All Men are Mortal*. Dismissed from teaching post over accusations of immorality.
1944	Play *Who Shall Die?* written and performed. Liberation of Paris (25 August). *Les Temps modernes* set up.
1945	World War II ends. *The Blood of Others* published.
1947	Lecture tour in US. Meets Nelson Algren and begins a passionate affair with him. *The Ethics of Ambiguity* published. Visits Algren in September.
1948	*America Day by Day* and *L'existentialisme et la sagesse des nations* published. Spends May to July with Algren in US.
1949	*The Second Sex* published. Algren visits Beauvoir in Paris. Begins work on *The Mandarins*.
1950	Spends August and September with Algren at his new house on Lake Michigan.
1951	Returns to Lake Michigan to see Algren in October – their affair ends. Buys first car.
1952	Breast cancer scare – operation for non-malignant tumour. Begins relationship with Claude Lanzmann.
1954	France defeated in Vietnam. Algerian War of Independence begins. *The Mandarins* published. Wins *Goncourt* Prize.
1955	*Must We Burn De Sade?* published. Buys a one-roomed flat overlooking Montparnasse Cemetery. Visits Moscow and China.
1956	First of many summers spent in Rome with Sartre. Begins writing memoirs.
1957	*The Long March* published.
1958	Beginning of the Fifth Republic. *Memoirs of a Dutiful Daughter* published. Becoming more involved in militant protests against the war in Algeria. End of relationship with Lanzmann.
1960	*The Prime of Life* published. Signs Manifesto of the 121 against French policy in Algeria. Visits Cuba and Brazil. Supports Djamila Boubacha. Meets Sylvie le Bon.
1962	Publication of Gisèle Halimi's book about the Djamila Boupacha case with preface by Beauvoir. Peace in Algeria.

1963	*Force of Circumstance* published. Mother, Françoise de Beauvoir dies. Develops closer relationship with Sylvie le Bon.
1964	*A Very Easy Death* published. Takes part in debate on the role of literature – *Que peut la littérature?* Algren breaks off correspondence.
1965	Begins writing *Les Belles Images* in the autumn.
1966	*Les Belles Images* published. Takes part in the Russell War Crimes Tribunal. Visits Japan.
1967	*The Woman Destroyed* completed in May. Russell War Crimes Tribunal continues.
1968	*The Woman Destroyed* published. Supports militant students in the protests in May.
1970	*Old Age* published. Defends press freedom. Supports women's movement and takes part in demonstration in favour of contraception and abortion.
1971	Signs 'Manifesto of the 343' declaring she has had an illegal abortion. Takes part in pro-abortion demonstration.
1972	*All Said and Done* published. Takes part in the meetings denouncing the crimes perpetrated against women. Works with *Choisir* (pro-choice organization). Takes part in Bobigny abortion trial.
1974	President of the *Ligue du droit des femmes*.
1975	Awarded the Jerusalem Prize in recognition of her promotion of the freedom of the individual.
1977	Director of journal *Questions féministes*.
1979	*When Things of the Spirit Come First* published.
1980	Sartre dies (15 April). Spends a month seriously ill in hospital with pneumonia. Adopts Sylvie le Bon.
1981	*Adieux: A Farewell to Sartre* published. Algren dies of a massive heart attack. Honorary Chair of the *Commission Femmes et Culture*.
1983	Sartre's *Lettres au Castor* published.
14 April 1986	Beauvoir dies after a short illness.
19 April 1986	Thousands attend Beauvoir's funeral.

GLOSSARY

Agrégation   Competitive postgraduate examination for teaching posts in *lycées* and universities.

Authenticity   When we acknowledge our freedom and take responsibility for our actions.

Bad faith   When we deny our freedom and refuse to accept responsibility for our actions or when we deny the givens of our situation.

Canon   Writings that are considered to be of lasting significance.

Consciousness   (Mind), the relation we have with the world.

Contingent   Something which occurs which might not have occurred.

Essence   Characteristics which define human nature.

Ethics   Philosophical inquiry into or theory of standards of right and wrong, good and bad in respect of character and conduct.

Existentialism   Philosophy according to which existence precedes essence and which insists on human freedom and responsibility.

Facticity   The givens of our situation.

Figurative   Language characterized by metaphor (when one thing is described as being another thing) and other figures of speech; the opposite of literal.

Focalizer   The character through whose perspective the story is presented.

For-itself   When we think of ourselves as transcendent consciousnesses, acknowledging our freedom and orienting ourselves towards things beyond ourselves.

Idealism   A worldview that places special value on ideas and ideals.

Immanence   When we think of ourselves as things in the world and are confined by the givens of our situation.

In-itself   When we think of ourselves as things in the world, the givens of our situation.

Intentionality   The relation between consciousness and real and imagined objects in the world.

Intersubjectivity   The philosophical problem of the existence of other minds.

Lycée   State secondary school.

Metaphysics   Philosophy to do with our relations with the world and other consciousnesses.

Narrative   The process of production of a text.

New Novel/New Novelists   The French writer Alain Robbe-Grillet led debate about the New Novel (*nouveau roman*) in the 1950s and 1960s. In his avant-garde, experimental anti-novels, traditional characteristics of the novel such as plot, characterization and narrative were rejected.

Omniscient   With total, God-like knowledge of the characters and their actions.

Ontology   The branch of philosophy concerned with being.

Other   The inessential, the subordinate.

Phenomenology   The philosophical method that attempts to describe our experience directly.

Phoney war   The period between the declaration of World War II and the German invasion of Western Europe (September 1939 – March 1940).

Project   What we choose to do in the world.

Reciprocity   When individuals or groups recognize each other's freedom and treat each other both as subject and object.

Rhetorical strategies   The ways in which writers choose to communicate their message.

Roman à clef   A novel in which the characters are thinly disguised representations of real people.

Story   A succession of events.

Subject   The essential, the sovereign.

Subjection   The struggle between individuals or groups for subjective domination.

Technocrat   A scientist, engineer, or other expert who is one of a group of similar people who have political power as well as technical knowledge.

Text   The discourse that tells a story.

Transcendence   Existence characterized by freedom and directed to what is beyond ourselves.

Women's condition   Women's position in society.

FURTHER READING

Major Works by Simone de Beauvoir

(French editions with original dates of publication are given first, then English editions referred to in the text, followed by the most recent English editions available, if different.)

L'Invitée, coll. folio, Paris: Gallimard, 1943. *She Came to Stay*, trans. Yvonne Moyse and Roger Senhouse, London: Fontana, 1982 (Harmondsworth: Penguin, 1990/New York: Norton, 1999)

Pyrrhus et Cinéas, Paris: Gallimard, 1944. Translation forthcoming: The Beauvoir Series, University of Illinois Press, eds. Sylvie Le Bon de Beauvoir and Margaret A. Simons

Le Sang des autres, coll. folio, Paris: Gallimard, 1945. *The Blood of Others*, trans. Yvonne Moyse and Roger Senhouse, Harmondsworth: Penguin, 1986 (2002)

Tous les hommes sont mortels, coll. folio, Paris: Gallimard, 1946. *All Men are Mortal*, trans. Leonard M. Friedman, Cleveland, Ohio: World Publishing, 1955 (London: Virago, 1995/New York: Norton, 1992)

Pour une morale de l'ambiguïté, coll. idées, Paris: Gallimard, 1947. *The Ethics of Ambiguity*, trans. Bernard Fretchman, New York: Citadel Press, 1976 (1986/New York: Carol Publishing Group, 1995)

L'Existentialisme et la sagesse des nations, including 'Idéalisme moral et réalisme politique', 'Littérature et métaphysique' and 'Œil pour œil', Paris: Nagel, 1948. Translation forthcoming: The Beauvoir Series, University of Illinois Press, eds. Sylvie Le Bon de Beauvoir and Margaret A. Simons

Le Deuxième Sexe, 2 vols., coll. folio, Paris: Gallimard, 1949. *The Second Sex*, trans. H. M. Parshley, Harmondsworth: Penguin, 1975 (London: Vintage, 1997)

Les Mandarins, coll. folio, Paris: Gallimard, 1954. *The Mandarins*, trans. Leonard M. Friedman, London: Fontana, 1977 (New York: Norton, 1999)

Mémoires d'une jeune fille rangée, coll. folio, Paris: Gallimard, 1958. *Memoirs of a Dutiful Daughter*, trans. James Kirkup, Harmondsworth: Penguin, 1965 (2001)

La Force de l'âge, Paris: Gallimard, 1960. *The Prime of Life*, trans. Peter Green, Harmondsworth: Penguin, 1988 (2001/New York: Avalon, 1994)

La Force des choses, 2 vols., Paris: Gallimard, 1963. *Force of Circumstance*, Trans. Richard Howard, Harmondsworth: Penguin, 1981 (1988)

Une Mort très douce, coll. folio, Paris: Gallimard, 1964. *A Very Easy Death*, trans. Patrick O'Brian, Harmondsworth: Penguin, 1983 (London: Methuen Educational, 1986/New York: Pantheon, 1985)

Les Belles Images, coll. folio, Paris: Gallimard, 1966. *Les Belles Images*, trans. Patrick O'Brian, London: Fontana, 1985

La Femme rompue, coll. folio, Paris: Gallimard, 1968. *The Woman Destroyed*, trans. Patrick O'Brian, London: Fontana, 1982 (New York: Pantheon, 1987)

Tout compte fait, coll. folio, Paris: Gallimard, 1972. *All Said and Done*, trans. Patrick O'Brian, New York: Paragon, 1993 (Harmondsworth: Penguin, 1991)

Lettres à Sartre, 2 vols., ed. Sylvie Le Bon de Beauvoir, Paris: Gallimard, 1990. *Letters to Sartre*, trans. and ed. Quintin Hoare, London: Vintage, 1993

Journal de guerre: septembre 1939–janvier 1941, ed. Sylvie Le Bon de Beauvoir, Paris: Gallimard, 1990. Translation forthcoming: The Beauvoir Series, University of Illinois Press, eds. Sylvie Le Bon de Beauvoir and Margaret A. Simons

Lettres à Nelson Algren, un amour transatlantique 1947–64, ed. Sylvie Le Bon de Beauvoir, Paris: Gallimard, 1997. *A Transatlantic Love Affair: Letters to Nelson Algren*, New York: The New Press, 1998

Books about Simone de Beauvoir

The following books, which were consulted in writing this Guide, are a good starting point for finding out more about Simone de Beauvoir's life and work.

Bair, Deirdre, *Simone de Beauvoir: A Biography*, London: Cape, 1990

Fallaize, Elizabeth, *The Novels of Simone de Beauvoir*, London: Routledge, 1988

Fallaize, Elizabeth, ed., *Simone de Beauvoir: A Critical Reader*, London: Routledge, 1998

Fullbrook, Edward and Kate Fullbrook, *Simone de Beauvoir: A Critical Introduction*, Cambridge: Polity, 1998

Mahon, Joseph, *Existentialism, Feminism and Simone de Beauvoir*, London: Macmillan, 1997

Moi, Toril, *Simone de Beauvoir: The Making of an Intellectual Woman*, Oxford: Blackwell, 1994

Schwarzer, Alice, *Simone de Beauvoir Today: Conversations 1972–1982*, trans. Marianne Howarth, London: Hogarth, 1984

Simons, Margaret A., *Beauvoir and 'The Second Sex': Feminsim, Race and the Origins of Existentialism*, Oxford: Rowman & Littlefield, 1999

Tidd, Ursula, *Simone de Beauvoir: Gender and Testimony*, Cambridge: Cambridge University Press, 1999

INDEX